THE **CRASH**

Overcoming when life falls apart...

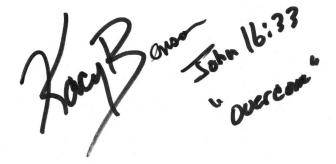

Kacy Benson
John 16:33
"Overcome"

KACY BENSON

Scripture quotations marked (MSG) are from THE MESSAGE, Copyright © by Eugene H. Peterson 1993, 1994, 1995, 1996, 2000, 2001, 2002. Used by permission of NavPress. All rights reserved. Represented by Tyndale House Publishers, Inc.

Scripture quotations marked (TLB) are taken from The Living Bible copyright © 1971. Used by permission of Tyndale House Publishers, Inc., Carol Stream, Illinois 60188. All rights reserved.

Scripture quotations marked (NLT) are taken from the Holy Bible, New Living Translation, © 1996, 2004, 2007, 2013, 2015 by Tyndale House Foundation. Used by permission of Tyndale House Publishers, Inc., Carol Stream, Illinois 60188. All rights reserved.

Scripture quotations marked (NIV) are taken from the Holy Bible, New International Version®, NIV®. Copyright © 1973, 1978, 1984, 2011 by Biblica, Inc.™ Used by permission of Zondervan. All rights reserved worldwide. www.zondervan.com The "NIV" and "New International Version" are trademarks registered in the United States Patent and Trademark Office by Biblica, Inc.™

Excerpt taken from *"Moms Raising Sons To Be Men"* © 2013 by Rhonda Stoppe Published by Harvest House Publishers Eugene, Oregon 97402. Used by permission.

Cover Photo by Christian Bruno - Used by Permission
under Creative Commons Zero (Public Domain)
Cover Design by Marcus Moore & Daniel Pitner
Interior Design & Layout by Debbie Bishop
Manuscript co-written by Frances Alcorn

THE CRASH

ISBN: 978-0-9860527-9-8 (Paperback)
ISBN: 978-0-9860527-8-1 (eBook)

Printed in the United States of America

Mpact Publishing
A Division of Mpact Events, LLC

Acknowledgements

The Crash is dedicated to my mom, Christy Benson, who did whatever it took to raise two boys on her own, and my grandma, Margie Benson, for always taking care of me. Your unconditional love and support for me through the good times and bad times will never be forgotten. I would not be who I am today without both of you.

Thank you to my wife and amazing mother to our children, Vickie. You have always believed in me and supported me in so many ways. I can never thank you enough for always being by my side.

Thank you Real Life staff and members for supporting this project in so many ways.

Thank you to numerous friends and supporters who have contributed through prayer, finances and encouragement.

Thank you Dave King for investing so much of your time, energy and interest in seeing this through.

Thank you Frances Alcorn for all your hard work, resourcefulness and collaboration in writing this book.

Finally, thank you to Mac, Valerie & Melissa Warren, and Sammy & Billie Joe O'Rear, for finding and staying with me on that dreadful day. I'm so glad we finally found all of you.

The Crash is written in memory of my grandfather,

James Wilburn Benson
1928 - 1977

Table of Contents

Acknowledgements   i

Introduction   vii

Chapter 1 - Mayday, Mayday, Mayday   1

Chapter 2 - Climbing Out of the Crash   15

Chapter 3 - The Knife   29

Chapter 4 - Wandering in the Woods   39

Chapter 5 - The Voice   61

Chapter 6 - Alone   75

Chapter 7 - The Fence   91

Chapter 8 - Rescued   113

Epilogue   137

Finding the Rescuers   147

East Texas Light   157

Introduction

The first time I met Kacy, we scheduled a one-hour lunch. The lunch turned into several hours as he began to share many of the stories you will read in this book. I had two thoughts as he shared. First, how did all of this happen to one guy? A close second, Kacy has to write this stuff down to reach more people with his life-changing message. My prayer is that you will be as inspired as I was when you read them in the pages that follow.

I have been fortunate to count Kacy as a friend for more than five years now. During that time, I have been blown away by everything this guy has endured and experienced. I have also seen firsthand how Kacy's life story has helped teenagers and adults find hope.

This book shares several amazing true stories from Kacy's life. I assure you, the stories are true and this guy is as real as it gets. You will be challenged, blessed, and encouraged as you read.

The Crash is more than a story. It is a journey we are all on. Jesus said that we all have an enemy that wants to steal our joy, kill our dreams, and destroy God's plan for us. Jesus also said His plan is to give us life that overflows. In each chapter of this book, you will see this struggle and feel this fight - but you will also see God's faithfulness and sense God's hand protecting, leading and guiding Kacy…just like He can for us all.

Whatever It Takes

Micah Davidson, Lead Pastor
Real Life Church, Austin, Texas

CHAPTER 1

Mayday, Mayday, Mayday

*Then call on me when you are in trouble, and
I will rescue you, and you will give me glory.*
~ Psalm 50:15 (NLT)

I jumped into the small airplane without hesitation.
I had done this with my grandparents many
times. But this hot August day in 1977 would
be different than anything I had yet experienced.
I was almost seven years old, excited about this trip, and
eager to once again spend time with my grandparents.
My grandpa, James Wilburn Benson, was an experienced
pilot and owned a small plane. The Mooney M80 was
a single engine plane that could hold up to four people
and I loved getting to fly with him. On this day, he and
my grandma had flown down to Galveston, Texas, where

my younger brother, Lancer and I lived with my mom. Mom had driven us to the small airstrip on the island where I hopped out of the car and quickly climbed aboard. I was ready to go! It would be a short trip by air to their home in Springhill, Louisiana.

I remember something that happened one time with my Grandpa. Like many times before, he took me to get ice cream. We arrived at an ice cream shop, and "apparently" I was allergic to chocolate. I decided anyways that I wanted chocolate ice cream, but my grandpa had gotten me vanilla. I didn't want vanilla, so I told him that. He said, "Well, you will have vanilla." So, I kicked him in the leg, and he kicked me back. I started crying, and my Grandma looked straight at my Grandpa. She asked him, "Wilburn, what did you do?' He said, "I kicked him." She asked "Why?" He said, "He kicked me first!" That is who this man was. He was not going to take mess from a five year old. Clearly, he had earned my respect, as well as my love. On this day in Galveston, I was anticipating another special visit . . . and maybe some more ice cream!

At the last moment, my mom snatched my brother from the plane. She suddenly felt that he wasn't quite old enough to go away without her. So, my grandpa started the engine, turned to taxi down the runway, and the three of us were on our way to Northern Louisiana. In my excitement, I never imagined the events awaiting me that day.

I remember sitting in my seat, looking around the cockpit, intrigued with all the "stuff" inside my grandpa's plane. I didn't know the names or purpose for all the buttons and lights around me, but there was a lot to take in. On the wall next to my head, I noticed an old yellow box with a very long antenna. My grandpa put on his headset, pushed a bunch of buttons, said some numbers, and we took off.

As the plane lifted, the Gulf Coast began to disappear from view. I began to see more fields, scattered lakes, and trees. Before long, we were passing over East Texas and our journey was more than halfway complete. In a short time, I had watched the scenery change from sand to wetlands, and now we looked down on the Piney Woods of East Texas as we soared through the sky toward our destination.

Suddenly the plane began to shudder, and my attention immediately went to my grandpa. The plane also began making crazy noises, and smoke was rolling from the front near the propeller. (*Later I learned that an oil line had cracked, spilling oil from the manifold onto the engine, which in turn had caught on fire.)*

Oil began spraying from the engine area up onto the windshield, and smoke was filling the cabin, making it hard to breath and still harder to see. All this happened so fast. I knew something was wrong, but I wasn't worried. My grandpa never panicked and I felt positive he had everything under control.

Then grandpa spoke into his headset, with sternness in his voice, "Mayday, mayday, mayday!" He was also spouting off coordinates, numbers, and so many other things that seemed to get mixed up in my head. I watched as he opened the side window, in an attempt to let out some of the smoke, because he couldn't see the controls. He couldn't see what lay ahead through the greasy windshield. So, he stuck his head out the window looking for a safe place to land the plane. The ground was barely visible below us.

At my young age, I couldn't comprehend the seriousness of our situation; and yet, I knew we were in trouble. I saw and smelled the oil and smoke. I knew my grandpa was in charge of the situation, even as I heard my grandma's desperate cry, "What's happening? What's happening?" And while she was frantically seeking answers from him, she would look back at me and shout, "Put your head down!"

I would duck my head down for a moment; but then I'd sit up again because I wanted to see what was going on. I wanted to see what was happening. But each time my head popped back up, she would turn back and yell, "Put your head down!" As we continued like this, my grandpa was trying to quiet her nerves. "Calm down, Calm down, I've got this…" I'll never forget how he held his composure in the midst of the turmoil, comforting my grandma with his words. All the while, he was circling a small pasture among the trees and looking out the window for a way to avoid disaster.

The shuddering was so intense that it felt like the plane was going to fly apart. My grandpa quickly turned back to tighten my seatbelt and pulled it really hard. He then reached for the yellow box by my head and flipped a switch that caused a loud beeping noise. I later learned this was a radio beacon that sends a distress signal to nearby airport towers. He was notifying air traffic control that we were about to land, or crash, or both! He clicked the beacon on and the loud beeping joined the crazy screams of the engine and my grandma's anxious cries. Then my grandpa once again called out into his headset "Mayday, mayday, mayday!" Those words will forever be engraved in my memory. I didn't know what that meant at the time. But he made that call over and over.

In later years, I found out that "mayday" is an international distress signal for mariners and aviators. It indicates that the caller is facing a life-threatening emergency. The call is given three times in a row, followed by a pause, and then yelled three times again. The triple repeat is so that people who give the call will not be misunderstood. (The original term "m'aider" is French for "help me.") It is actually a federal offense to yell "Mayday!" into a public address system or pilot's system if there is not an actual plane crash or emergency situation. These words are to be taken very seriously, as a matter of life or death.

When I learned the meaning of this phrase, it immediately brought back the memory of that dramatic day with my grandparents, together in that plane as we circled the pasture frantically trying to land. I can still hear my grandpa's voice repeating, "Mayday, mayday, mayday."

It all happened quickly. Emotions were tense and I felt the stress, but no fear. I felt like my grandpa was in control, even though it appeared that we were going down and my grandma was panicking. He had such peace and confidence about him. He wasn't yelling, except to repeat that solemn call for help over the radio. "Mayday, mayday, mayday. We are going down!" He could see what was coming, but he didn't lose his head. Instead, he simply delivered a sincere cry for help. We desperately needed help!

I understand this now on a much larger scale. After being in the ministry for over twenty years, I see people every day who are in trouble and calling out their own "mayday." I meet both youth and adults and I hear them crying out in many different ways, and for many different reasons. Some cry out because they're in pain; others cry out because of loss, or fear, confusion or depression. The world is in distress and people are crying out. I also see those who should be crying out— but they remain silent.

One of my favorite stories from the Bible is about a blind man named Bartimaeus. The setting is Jericho.

> *As Jesus and his disciples, together with a large crowd, were leaving the city, a blind man named Bartimaeus was sitting by the roadside begging.*
> *~ Mark 10:46 (NIV)*

There are a lot of people who are blind in this world.

People living blindly, not necessarily in regard to physical sight, but who are not seeing what they need to see to survive and succeed spiritually. They may be looking for help, just like Bartimaeus, who was on the side of the road begging when he heard that Jesus of Nazareth was coming by. The next verse states that he began to SHOUT (one Bible translation says "cry out"), "Jesus, Son of David, have mercy on me!" Bartimaeus recognized he needed help.

But here's the crazy part of the story. In verse 48, it says that many rebuked him and told him to be quiet. "Shut up," they said, "Stop yelling; stop crying out." Sometimes those around us try to stop our cries for help. They say that it isn't "cool" to cry out, or "You're not a man if you cry out. Don't ask for help; you should be able to handle life on your own." They will mock those who need help, because they don't want help, don't want to help anyone else, and many times are incapable of offering help—even if they wanted to.

> *"I cry out to God; yes, I SHOUT. Oh, that God would listen to me!"* ~ *Psalm 77:1 (NLT)*

So because of peer pressure, or embarrassment, or so many other reasons, people suffer in silence. They keep their hurt to themselves. They are headed for disaster and ruin, yet the people around them urge them to be quiet.

Bartimaeus wasn't just spiritually blind; he was physically blind as well. He was hurting and in desperate need. He was aware of how helpless he was on his own. But, when he heard the news that the Lord was right there on his road, he recognized Jesus as his chance for rescue, and he put out his own "mayday" cry. Instead of listening to the crowd who tried to shush him, (and here's why I love this story), verse 48 tells us that he "shouted all the more!" In essence his message was, "I don't care what these people are saying, I need you, Jesus!"

At that plea, Jesus stopped and said, "Call him over." Interestingly, the crowd then changed their tune. They turned to the blind man and said, "Hey, cheer up! Get on your feet, man. Jesus wants to talk to you."

Of course, Bartimaeus jumped up and went to Jesus, who asked, "What do you want me to do for you?" and the blind man replied simply, "I want to see." Jesus responded, "Go. Your faith has healed you." Immediately, Bartimaeus received his sight and he began to celebrate Jesus and follow him.

"Lord, help!" they cried in their trouble, and He saved them from their distress."

~Psalm 107:28 (NLT)

Now, this blind man was rescued because he cried out in his distress, and Jesus heard him. Jesus will hear you, too. How many times should we be yelling "mayday" and we don't because we listen to the crowd? Or, on the other hand, we may be the ones telling those who are crying out to be quiet.

At times, people may be in distress and crying out for help, but we don't hear them. Or we hear them, but we're not really listening. For example:

When I was growing up in Galveston, my mom was raising us two boys on her own. Sometimes, she worked two jobs just so she could take care of us, but we were free to run around the neighborhood just like any kids. We weren't out looking for trouble— just having fun. We lived near the beach, and often watched people parasailing, a sport in which a person is attached to a great big parachute and a towrope. The rope is attached to a boat that speeds along while the person is let up into the air. It's a fun ride I had seen many times, but I had never been able to do it.

So, here I was with my friends one day and we found a huge piece of plastic—the sort of thing that you might come across on a construction site. Anyway, we had this incredible piece of plastic and, since it is very windy down on the gulf coast, I had a brilliant idea. "Let's make a parasail!" So, my friends and I got together and constructed this parachute-like apparatus. We tied each of the four corners of the plastic to a rope. Then we fastened the rope at the middle, and also around the waist of one of our friends. We had another rope that acted as a guide. Then, we waited for the wind to do its thing.

This is what kids do at the age of 11 or 12 years old. Right? We built a parachute and we were on a part of the beach where the wind really gusts. And this poor kid had this piece of plastic tied to him. I was holding one part of the rope and another guy was holding the other part. And the wind cooperated with a "whoosh," lifting our friend off the ground. We began to let out the rope. (I can only imagine what this guy's mother would have been thinking if she had known what was happening.) We let out more and more of the rope until he was about as far up as he could go, and we were just holding on watching him fly. He was way up in the air, parasailing! And we were proud because we had done it. He was having a really great time! We were

11

sure of it. He was screaming, and although we couldn't really hear what he was saying, to us it sounded like, "Ah, ha-ha-ha-ha!" We congratulated ourselves for our success, knowing that he was having a blast flying through the air. "Yeah, he loves it!" We thought.

But then, it looked like he was still yelling, but we couldn't hear any sounds coming from him. At that moment we accidentally let the rope go. We had been trying to let him get up a little higher, but the rope slipped from our hands and he started to head out towards the Gulf of Mexico. We all ran after that rope and dived on top of it, pulling him back down to the ground. It was only then that we realized that he couldn't breathe and we were trying to figure out what was wrong. It didn't take long to discover that the rope had slipped up around his mid-section, and cut off the breath in his lungs. He had been yelling to try to tell us he was in trouble from the first. We had totally misunderstood his cries. We thought he was having fun and since we couldn't hear clearly, we dismissed his cries for help.

And that's what we do sometimes when we're walking through the streets, going to work or school, and there are people around us crying out. We walk on by. We put our own interpretation on their cry. We want to believe all is well, so we miss it.

How can we recognize a "mayday" call? People cry out in different ways. They cry out with their attitudes. They cry out with drug and alcohol use. They cry out through their actions. People even cry out through words. We get so caught up in our own lives, that we fail to listen, or we miss the "mayday" cry or fail to identify it for what it is. But the fact is, that people are crying out and, as Christians, God wants us to hear and run to help those who are calling out.

What do we need to do to hear those who are crying out? How do we allow the Lord to use us to help reach out to those who cry?

What distress signals are you sending in your own life? When you feel like you're going down, who do you cry "mayday" to? What does it look like or sound like when you call? And who in this world is listening, anyway? One thing is certain, God always listens and is always ready to rescue.

> *Is anyone crying for help? God is listening, ready to rescue you. If your heart is broken you'll find God right there. If you're kicked in the gut, he'll help you catch your breath.* ~ *Psalm 34:17 (NLT)*

CHAPTER 2

Climbing Out of the Crash

"He comforts us in all of our troubles,
so that we can comfort others when they are troubled,
we'll be able to give them the same comfort
that God has given us.
~ 2 Corinthians 1:4 (MSG)

It was obvious we were going down. Grandpa had repeatedly called for help. He was having trouble seeing the gauges through all the smoke in the cockpit, and he had to act fast. Despite all of his efforts to land safely and smoothly, the plane and gravity had their own way and we overshot the pasture beneath us. Instead of approaching the clearing at a safe angle, we came diving toward earth like a rock, hitting the ground really fast and really hard!

When the plane struck the ground, we immediately bounced back up into the tree line. That single bounce sent the plane airborne again and we formed a ragged path into the woods. As we roughly crashed through the trees, the wings came off, the sides of the plane were torn away, and the roof lifted from above our heads, so that we were suddenly aware of everything outside the plane.

So much of the plane had been ripped away, that we were entirely exposed. Branches smacked us from both sides. My grandpa's head hit against a tree. I don't know how many miles per hour we were traveling, but it seemed that we kept sliding forever through the woods. And then, everything suddenly stopped.

The luggage in the back, however, still had a lot of momentum and it kept moving, along with bits of metal and other fragments—all of which struck me in the back of the head. At this point, my seat belt popped off, completely broken, and I fell forward between the front and back seats (which probably saved my life). The luggage, airplane pieces, and tree limbs crashed down behind me sending my head forward into the seat in front of me. I was knocked unconscious.

When I awoke, I found myself buried beneath the

debris. Amazed that I was still alive, I wondered what would happen next. I remember lying still, not wanting to move. Did I have it in me to fight my way out of this heap? I was small; I was scared. It was overwhelming. At six years old, I had to make the decision to get up and get out, or give in and stay stuck. I chose to fight for survival.

So I wiggled and squirmed. I pushed and pulled to get loose from the wreckage and crawl out from the crash. Little by little, I struggled out of the rubble. Once my head emerged, I saw that my grandparents were helpless. When I was finally able to stand up, all I could see was ruin. My grandpa's neck was broken, and he was lying on top of my grandma and couldn't move. Her seatbelt had cut her body almost completely in half. But, for now at least, they were both still breathing. The airplane, however, was torn to shreds.

I was shocked by the mess, but very glad to be alive. I had not caused the crash. I didn't want to be a part of it. However, I had been trapped in the middle of it. Looking back at the wreckage, I wondered why it had happened.

I don't wonder so much anymore. If we are honest with ourselves, we have all experienced some sort of "crash" or tragedy in our lives. Whether self inflicted, or by someone else's hand, things happen to us that take our conscious efforts to overcome. Even if you have never been in an airplane accident, you may find yourself having to crawl out from life's wreckage on any given day.

When huge pressures weigh us down, we have to choose to shake off those crushing burdens ... If our plans fail, and our hopes and dreams have crumbled, we have to climb out of the crash ... If a storm has torn our world apart, we can't lie under the rubble playing the "poor me" game. There is help. There is a way to be free. But we have to choose whether to stay stuck or to climb out.

My mom demonstrated this while raising my brother and me. She always did her best for us, working hard to keep food on the table and a roof overhead. We lived in small apartments and just anywhere we could at that time. My dad was not around to help, so she did what she could to take care of us on her own.

It seemed impossible to get ahead. Nothing was going to change without long hours of work and great effort. Finally she got a break, when a friend decided to sell her a trailer house. That was a step up for us. My mom sacrificed everything to buy this trailer, and we moved out to a place on Galveston Island called Eight Mile Road. We made the move in the late spring of 1983.

After so many years in crowded apartments and urban housing, it was nice to have a little breathing room. The property was not even an acre, but it was ours. My best memory of our new home was what was under my feet. There had never been a lawn in any of the places we had lived, so standing in the grass was a new and exciting experience. We now had a place of our own, where I had the comfort—or, as I felt, the luxury—of walking outside barefooted in the grass.

That was a memorable time. We enjoyed our new home. I played baseball that summer and life was good. But storms will come, and one was headed our way, literally.

On August 15th, Hurricane Alicia began forming in the Atlantic, moving toward the Gulf of Mexico. At this point we didn't really know where it would hit—Louisiana, Mexico, Corpus Christi, Brownsville, or elsewhere—and we didn't really know how bad it would be.

Two days later, Alicia had strengthened to a Category

2 hurricane, and by the time it made landfall at 3:00 am August 18th, it had become a Category 3 major hurricane, with winds of 115 mph. For so many days, it had hovered out in the Gulf, and eventually it began to make its way straight into Galveston.

My mom made a quick decision to get off the island. We didn't have money to go very far. We went to our Aunt's house in Houston to ride it out. Even on the mainland the storm was extremely heavy—and deadly. In total, it took the lives of 21 people and caused around $2.6 billion in damage.

Of course, we were worried about what might be happening to our trailer. We had been forced to leave in a hurry, so we left a lot of things behind. My mother still regrets that she didn't think to grab the baby pictures. She has very few pictures of my brother and me, and this was a sad thing, but at the time she was just concerned with getting us out with our lives. We were safe, but hoped that we would still have a home to go back to. Finally, the storm passed through, and we were able to return to the island.

As we drove home, we encountered many barriers that we had to get over and around in order to reach the trailer. For instance, one road was blocked by a downed telephone pole. Another had a tree across it. So we worked our way around these hurdles, coming up on the far side of the road where we could finally see the trailer. We had held our breath up until the moment we could see the wall standing. At that moment we celebrated. We were in the car cheering, "It made it… it didn't go down!"

There was so much junk scattered in the roadway that we had to park the car two hundred yards away; the roads were impassable. Once again we had to get around the debris in the streets—this time on foot. We climbed over trees and lots of other wreckage as we made our way toward our home.

We were so excited that our humble trailer had survived the storm. The joy of that realization kept us going as we climbed over all the debris and obstacles in our path. When we came around the corner, our hearts sank. Instead of four walls and a roof, we were met with nothing but empty sky. "I cant' believe it. It's gone," and we stood there in shock. It had all been an optical illusion. The one wall we had seen from a distance was all that remained. Everything else was gone. Completely gone. We had lost everything we owned in a single day.

I fell to my knees in the grass that I used to love—the grass that had been under my bare feet just a few short days before. But now, that was no consolation. Instantly, the tears poured from my eyes with the realization that we had lost all that we had. My family had nothing now, it seemed.

In the middle of my pity party, my mom walked over to me and said, "Listen. We can't just cry about it. We're going to have to pick ourselves up and move on."

And that attitude taught me a valuable lesson in that tragic moment. My mom was right. It was just like when I made the decision to pull myself out of that plane crash. Crying was not going to help the situation; we needed to move forward.

So we had a little cry and then we said, "All right! Let's recover what we can." Then we rummaged through the wreckage and salvaged what we could. There were a few things that had survived, but not much. Regardless, my mother's attitude was: "We're going to make it; we're going to be okay." We moved back to the apartments where we had lived before, and my mom worked hard, and I learned another great lesson: The storm happened, and it wasn't my fault. I was not responsible for bringing it—however, I was responsible for my reaction.

When we face storms or crashes in our lives, we can wallow, or we can crawl out of the rubble. As my mom said, "We can't cry now, we've got to save what we can, and we will be all right." Those words brought me comfort when I felt everything was lost. And that's what God does with us, when we are under pressure; when life is a wreck and we're buried in it all, God says, "I've got you. You're going to be okay. With My help, you can crawl out of anything."

But God does more than that. Crawling out isn't easy. When the twin towers went down during the 9-11 disaster in New York, there were many who had to make decisions to stay in the rubble or climb out over boulders, rubbish, and pieces of broken buildings, while choking on dust and struggling for life. Crawling out may seem impossible, but when we realize that we are unable to rescue ourselves, God reassures us. God's promises encourage us that even though things are falling apart, He is right there to help us.

"But we are hard pressed on every side, but not crushed... perplexed, but not in despair, persecuted but not abandoned, struck down but not destroyed, we always carry around in our bodies the death of Jesus so that the life of Jesus may also be revealed in our bodies."
~ *2 Corinthians 4:8-9 (NIV)*

We sometimes go through storms, so we can show this to others: He has helped me out of the rubble—out of the wreckage—and I, in turn, can help others.

I heard a story that really challenged me to help people who have been through similar situations in life as me. There was a man that fell into a hole. The man cried out for help to everyone who passed by.

The first person to hear his cries was a rich man. Somehow, he felt that he could help the suffering man by giving him money, so he walked over to the hole, pulled $100 out of his pocket, dropped it down into the hole and shouted, "Buy yourself a ladder!" That did not help the man get out of the hole.

The second man to pass by was a Christian. The poor guy in the hole looked up to him thinking, "Well, there is a righteous man of God. Surely, he can help me out!"

The Christian walked over to the hole, said a prayer for the man, and called out, "See you in church!" as he walked away, but the man in the hole remained stuck in the hole.

Finally, the man's friend came to the hole. The man in the hole called out, "Hey, Dave! It's me, Mike! Can you help me out?" So his friend, Dave walked over to the hole, and jumped down in beside him. The man was astonished. He looked at Dave as if he were crazy and said, "Dude! Why did you do that? Now we're both stuck down in this hole! What good is that?" And Dave replied, "Well listen... I jumped down because I've been here before, and I know the way out!"

The truth is, when we go through these stormy events, it enables us to help others who are going through them, as well. The friend who came to the man's aid when he was stuck in the hole is a solid representation of what Jesus has done for us. He came down to where we are, because he knew we couldn't bring ourselves up on our own.

> *"He comes alongside of us when we go through hard times, and before you know it he brings us alongside someone else who is going through hard times, so that we can be there for that person just as God was there for us..."*
> ~ *2 Corinthians 1:4 (MSG)*

You may be lying in rubble, wishing you could climb out, but it just seems too hard. It IS hard. Whether someone has done something to you, or if you created the situation on your own, it's not easy to get out. Maybe you face the rubble of depression. Maybe the rubble comes from someone's words that have hurt you. Maybe it's the wreckage that surrounds a financial crisis. No matter how the trouble is manifest in your life, in order to climb out, you have to CHOOSE to climb out. Ultimately you've got to stand up. And then you will discover that God has ahold of you and is pulling the debris away. Get up. Pull yourself out. Keep looking up. Stay focused on the goal.

I love this illustration: When people are climbing mountains, they seem to climb with greater energy when they can see the peak that they aspire to reach. When they can see the top of the mountain, they climb faster and more efficiently, but whenever the clouds cover the top of the mountain, they slow down. They are more likely to quit if they can't see the summit: they get sick, they get discouraged, or they decide not to climb anymore. There is something about seeing the top, having your eye on the goal, or looking at the place you are supposed to go that helps you keep going.

So stay focused. Keep your eyes upward and continue

to press on. Place your hope in the Lord. He is the one who gives us strength to dig out of the rubble, to climb out of the wreckage, and ultimately take "wings" to soar like an eagle. It's something to hang onto.

> *Isaiah 40:31 (NIV) promises: "But those who hope in the LORD will renew their strength. They will soar on wings like eagles; they will run and not grow weary, they will walk and not be faint."*

When our soaring plane crashed, God gave me the strength to emerge from the wreckage. But first, I made the choice to crawl out, and then I had another decision to make—I had to go find help.

CHAPTER 3

The Knife

The Lord is good to those whose hope is in him,
to the one who seeks him;
it is good to wait quietly for the salvation of the Lord.
~ Lamentations 3:25-26 (NIV)

When I awoke, buried in the wreckage of the plane crash, I saw a light filtering through the rubble to guide me out. Once I was safely out, I realized it was critical that I help my grandparents who couldn't help themselves. I heard my grandma moaning and my grandpa was crumpled over her lap, and he was having trouble moving. I knew they were both alive, but they were in bad shape.

In spite of his mangled condition, my grandpa still

seemed to be in charge. He told me that I needed to find his pocketknife, so that I could cut the seatbelt off of my grandma. I quickly began looking for the knife. I walked all around the perimeter of the crash, thinking it might be somewhere on the ground. I looked through the wreckage several times, and returned more than once to dig in his pockets, but it was nowhere to be found.

I looked everywhere, but I just could not find that knife. I felt helpless. I was sure that if I couldn't cut my grandma free, she was going to die. The whole situation was very stressful and scary. Being in a plane crash at six years old was an ordeal in itself, but then to feel that I was responsible for whether my grandma lived or died was almost more than I could stand. My grandpa said, "You've got to cut her seatbelt off," and I kept telling myself, "I have to find that pocketknife!" I was ready to panic.

My grandpa also suggested that I go find help, so I left the crash site repeatedly, searching for someone who might come to our aid. I wandered around for what seemed like hours, but all I saw were trees in the woods and cows in the pasture, which only scared me more (being a city kid) and made me run back again to check on my grandparents. While I was away from the plane, my grandpa had moved off of my grandma's lap, most likely because he thought he was hurting her. His neck was broken, and moving was just too much for him. On one of my trips back to the crash site, I found him dead. I was terrified, and I was afraid my grandma would also die, so I began another hard search for that knife, so that I could "save" her. Adrenaline rushed through my body, and my heart was pounding out of my chest as I searched everywhere for that knife.

Without a doubt, this matter was beyond what I could handle on my own. I wasn't a Christian at the time; I wasn't praying. However in my heart I was begging, "Somebody help me! I need some help on this!" And still, I couldn't find that knife!

> *"Wait for the Lord; be strong and take heart and wait for the Lord."* ~Psalm 27:14 (NIV)

On July 29th, 2000, I married Vickie, my amazing wife, soul mate and partner for life. It was a beautiful day. We were looking forward to our new life together, with all the hopes and dreams of young love. We expected to become a happy family, complete with the joy of children sometime in the future. We weren't planning to have a baby right away, but we were not surprised when we found out at the end of August that Vickie was pregnant. I was nervous, because I had no idea how to be a dad, but I could see how happy my wife was at the thought of being a mother. We started to plan.

First we prepared the nursery. Then, we started picking out names for either boy or girl. We prayed that the baby would be healthy, and we prayed that we would be good parents.

At Vickie's first appointment, the doctor projected a date of June 6, 2001, as the day we would say hello to our first-born child. We were actually going to be parents. The idea was becoming real to us. We shared our exciting news with family and friends and became more and more involved in planning for this new little member of our household.

A few weeks later, Vickie saw the doctor again. She returned home with sadness all over her face. The doctor had said that the baby wasn't growing the way it should. He wanted to monitor Vickie a little more closely. So she began going in every week to have tests run and to check the progress of the baby. Something was wrong, but I just didn't get it at the time. I remember lying in bed at night, with my hands on her belly, praying that this baby would grow.

Meanwhile, the doctor was doing his best to prepare us for the idea that she could miscarry any day. We refused to believe it, and prayed harder. "Lord, please let this baby live." We just knew that God would rescue our child. Crazy as it seemed, we were trying to reason things out with God. "Look, God. We love you. We're doing everything for you; we tell everyone about you. So, please do this thing for us," we would rationalize. People have a tendency to do that when we want something. I kept begging God to make everything better and I really believed He wouldn't let me down. I had great confidence that God would not let that baby die. He was going to take care of this.

Vickie was almost three months along in the pregnancy. On November 12th, 2000, I remember kissing my wife as I walked out the door to go speak at an event. I was on my way to do what I've always done—to tell people my story—sharing Jesus and witnessing for Him. I had no idea that while I was speaking, Vickie miscarried our first baby. When I came off stage, I called to check on her and she told me what had happened. She was weeping, and I didn't really know what to say. That was the hardest part—not having the words or the way to console her. I said what I thought I was supposed to say, "Everything is going to be all right." We hung up, and I headed home. But everything was not all right.

On my drive home, I began to question God. I didn't understand. We had prayed so hard for that baby, and I was doing everything I could for the Lord. I had just watched dozens of people find salvation, and I was confused. I felt that we had been obedient and faithful to God, and I wasn't entirely sure He had treated us right. In fact, I was angry. "I don't get it," I cried. "Your Word says to pray. And I prayed. How could you let this happen? We do so much for you and all I asked was this one thing…" I was mad, I was sad, I felt hurt, and I felt so sorry for Vickie. I didn't know how to behave with her. I'm a fixer. If something is broken I want to repair it. All she really needed was for me to just be there for her in her time of hurt, but I wanted to "fix it", and I couldn't.

That was the beginning of the most difficult time Vickie and I have ever had as a couple. There was a huge strain on our marriage. It was the first real test we had encountered together. We began to pull apart in our pain, fear, and anger. We didn't understand what God was doing, and we didn't know how to respond to each other. The distance between us became a gulf.

Later, when the baby's expected day of birth came around—June 6, 2001—Vickie and I were at a summer camp together. We had been emotionally detached since November. We loved each other, and we were surviving, but something was missing and we both knew it. We had not fully dealt with our feelings, and suddenly, the emotional dam gave away. During the worship time that evening, we both finally broke—first separately, and then together.

We were in two different parts of the room, on opposite sides of the building. I was one of the speakers preaching during the week. There I was, in the crowd, but I felt alone, as I stood bawling my eyes out. At the same time she was against the other wall bawling her eyes out. Dave King, the Camp Director, saw me crying. He had also seen my wife sobbing in another part of the room, and with a little reflection he approached me. "Hey. You look pretty broken here," he said, "And you might want to go check on your wife."

So, I pulled myself together, having no idea what had brought about her tears. I thought perhaps it was the worship message. I wasn't sure what was going on, but I went to her and put my arms around her. I was still crying. Up to this point, we had never dealt with our feelings, but now we began to pray together.

We asked God to forgive us for not trusting Him, and He began to comfort us both regarding the events of the past seven months. He began to restore our marriage and heal our hearts.

On August 19th, Vickie's birthday, and nearly a year from the time that we discovered she was first pregnant, we learned she was pregnant for the second time. Now we had to surrender all our fears and worries about that pregnancy to God. We had to trust Him completely even if things did not turn out as we expected. On May 20th, 2002, our second child Coleton was born, and on March 25th, 2005, our third child, Tyton would come around.

> *"There is a time for everything, and a season for every activity under the heavens." - Eccl. 3:1 (NIV)*

Sometimes, we think that what we want is what is best. We don't understand why God does what he does. When we were suffering through the loss of that first baby, we had no clue what God was doing. Vickie and I wanted that baby more than anything. It hurt deeply to lose that child, and the months that followed were painfully difficult. God had a plan for our lives through it all. We may never completely understand all the reasons things happen the way they do, and we no longer ask those questions. We accept that God is already there in our future. As trials occur, we cannot see the end. Looking back, there are some things we are able to grasp. For instance, in our case, if that baby had lived, we probably would not have been blessed with Coleton and Tyton. I honestly cannot imagine life without these boys. I am so grateful.

I am sure we all know someone whose parents have gotten cancer, or a husband or wife that may have contracted a fatal disease. We have watched as they prayed sincerely, believing God would rescue the loved one, who died in spite of their prayers. Then they asked "Why?"

I can't answer those tough questions; that's where trust comes in—having faith in the face of tragedy. When it seems that the Lord doesn't answer our prayers, we still need to be able to say, "God, I love you. God, You know better than I do."

So when I'm tempted to think that what I want is best, or I don't understand why God is doing things a certain way, I am reminded of my search for my grandpa's pocketknife. I wanted so badly to find that knife. I was certain that I needed it to save my grandma. Then I was later told that if I had cut the seatbelt off of her, she would have died almost immediately. The seatbelt was holding her together, and cutting it off would have caused her to bleed to death. I began to understand that we don't always know what is best for us. I am thankful that I couldn't find the knife.

Only God knows the end from the beginning. 2 Peter 3:8 reads, *"But do not forget this one thing, dear friends; With the Lord a day is like a thousand years, and a thousand years are like a day."* When God is looking at your life, he can see the whole book cover to cover; meanwhile, we're on one page. I later learned that the knife I searched for over and over was actually in my grandpa's pocket. I have no idea how I wasn't able to find it. The knife was given to me, and I still have it today. I keep it as a reminder to me of this message from an old Garth Brooks song, *"Some of God's greatest gifts are unanswered prayers..."* I had to learn that lesson—a very important lesson that continues to repeat itself in various phases throughout life.

CHAPTER 4

Wandering in the Woods

I sought the Lord and He answered me,
and delivered me from all my fears.
~ Psalm 34:4 (NIV)

Everyone has to deal with an emotion called fear. Sometimes your fears just get right in your face and you have no choice but to confront them. After my failed attempts to find the pocketknife anywhere in the wreckage, on the ground, or in my grandpa's pocket, I was FULL of fear. In fact, I was pretty "freaked out" about the whole crash. I didn't know what would happen to my grandparents, but I knew their future depended on me. That's a big load for a little kid to carry.

I felt like a failure since I couldn't find the knife, but my grandpa also persuaded me to go find help for my grandma. The thoughts in my head were "Are you kidding? I've got to walk through these woods?" I was in a strange place to begin with; and the whole woods setting was foreign to me. I was scared. I didn't know what was out there, but I knew I had to go.

I remember having a kind of awareness that my grandpa knew he was going to die. Even at six years old, I somehow understood this. He kept slipping in and out of consciousness. But during his alert moments, he kept saying, "Your grandma needs help . . . your grandma needs help . . . No matter what, you've got to find help for your grandma!" He was seriously concerned about her, encouraging me to do what I could to save her—first by looking for the pocketknife, and then by going on a search for someone who could help her. In all of this, he never said a word about himself or about my getting help for him.

At one point, I thought my grandma had died, because I couldn't see her breathing, and she wasn't saying anything. She was unconscious, but then she would wake up moaning or saying my name, and I was reassured, "Okay, she's awake, and I need to go find help." And my grandpa confirmed it. "Go, get help, son."

I had no choice. No matter how terrified I was, I had to go. So I left them. I had no idea which way to go or where I might find help. All I could see was debris—trees, wreckage and more trees. I began to guess where to go, and finally decided on what seemed to be the right direction, and started walking.

The first time out, I made my way by following the line of wreckage, because I remembered that the plane had bounced in the field before it tore through the trees. So I backtracked. I don't know how far I walked. It may not have been more than a hundred yards into the woods. As I went, I saw pieces of the plane and knocked-down trees, which created a trail of sorts, which led me out of the dense woods.

Eventually, I came upon a large pasture; it was the "little field" I had seen from the air—the one in which we had hoped to land. It didn't seem quite so small now. My mind was really blown when I came to the clearing. Here was something I had never seen before—at least, not up close. "Oh, wow," I thought as I stood facing a field of giant cows.

There were cows everywhere. I can only guess that they had heard the crash and were coming to investigate. When cows see people, they think, "Hey, we're going to get fed," so, they all gathered around me expectantly. To me it was more than intimidating; I was crazy with fear. I was from the city, I had never seen cows, and I really didn't know what these animals were all about. Would they bite me? Kick me? They were like giant dogs, and I didn't know how to react. But my love for my grandma pushed me forward in my search for help.

The cows were probably the BIGGEST part of my adventure. It was the first time I'd ever seen cows up close, and to me they were terrifying. And they were staring me down, as if I was there to give them food— or maybe I WAS the food. And when I took a few steps, they tagged right along behind me, adding to my fear, "Hey, these giant things are following me. They're freaking me out. Why won't they leave me alone?"

I didn't want to go through the fence into the pasture until the cows went away; so I ran up and down the fence line, getting torn up by the barbed wire. Everytime I stopped, there they were. They followed me back and forth. And it was so-so-so scary. Eventually they would leave and sit under a tree chewing their cuds, and I could venture out. When I found nothing—no one to help us—I would return to the plane to see if my grandparents were all right.

In what felt like an entire day, I tried to find help. I repeatedly made the trip out of the woods, lost my way, and had to face my fear.

Fear is a very real thing. It can freeze us in our tracks and keep us from doing what we need to do. Maybe, if I hadn't been so afraid as I wandered around, I would have been able to find help sooner. I know that my fear kept me from going into that cow pasture. The giant cows were only a part of the story.

While I was still in the woods, I kept seeing a piece of one of the wings from the plane. It was lodged up in the trees. Now, remember, I was walking through the Piney Woods of East Texas. Piney woods are, naturally, full of Pine trees. So, a wing sitting on a pine branch is very noticeable. As I walked back and forth, I kept noticing this wing sticking up, looking like it was about to fall on my head, and I told myself, "Do NOT go under the wing." And, I would walk around the tree to avoid walking under the wing hanging overhead. The way it was stretched across the treetops, I was sure it could fall on me. I had just survived this crash and didn't want any more trouble, so I kept telling myself, "Don't go under it ... don't go under it."

I was SO afraid of going under that tree that I got lost

in my fear. I had wandered so long, searching for help, but having no idea how or where to go. Then, suddenly, I gave in to exhaustion. Tired, hungry, scared, and unsure what to do next, I stopped to rest. I leaned against a tree and closed my eyes for just a moment. As I stood there resting, I happened to glance upward and my heart jumped. The one tree I had picked to lean up against was the one dangling the big wing above my head. It was about 30 to 40 feet up in the air. I jumped and ran. I had to move fast.

As I tried desperately to find someone—anyone—I couldn't get the image of my grandparents out of my mind. It really terrified me, seeing them broken up like this; these were my grandparents. They loved me, and I loved them. Seeing them hurt and unable to move was a horrible experience. I don't remember seeing any blood, which doesn't make sense, because apparently there was plenty. I guess my mind blocked it out. I'm sure I must have seen it; I just don't remember. I do remember seeing their limp forms all crumpled up in this heap of twisted wreckage. It was an awful mental picture for a little boy to carry around in those woods.

The definition of fear is this: *A strong unpleasant emotion caused by actual or perceived danger.* In my situation there was real (or actual) danger: the wing in the tree, and my grandparents fighting for their lives after the crash. There was also the perceived danger: the fear of the unknown, of being so alone, and the cattle that kept stalking me.

I thought the trees were monsters, for one thing. I looked up at them and they appeared to my mind like a scene from The Wizard of Oz. I had recently seen that movie and apparently it left an impression on me. I looked up into the pine trees and saw big gnarly creatures with arms reaching out to get me. Of course that was not real, but my young mind didn't know that.

Then of course, there were the cows. Looking back now, I am pretty sure they were not planning to eat me. At 6 years old, I didn't know that, and it seemed possible that they could hurt me in some way. I thought there was a real chance they might like to have me for lunch.

There are all types of fears. Some seem very silly, especially if we are not the one facing the fear. Many of these fears have their own names:

- Arachnophobia is the fear of spiders.
- Acrophobia is the fear of heights.
- Bananaphobia is the fear of bananas. There are actually people who are afraid of bananas.

- Coulrophobia, of course is a very legitimate fear. It's the fear of clowns.

It seems as though everybody's afraid of clowns these days. I am. I'm afraid of clowns—for what I think is a very good reason.

One summer there was a big parade in Springhill, Louisiana, where my mother's parents also lived. I was on the sidelines, watching everybody go by.

My mom's dad was a member of the Shriners organization. He was all dressed up in his Shriner outfit, complete with the tasseled hat. He and his Shriner brothers were about to come through the parade on noisy little motorcycles. It was to be one of their typical performances; they roar in on these miniature bikes, doing wheelies and other stunts. I was standing there waiting to see him. He was just about to come down the road toward me.

At that moment, I looked up and I saw this giant, ridiculously tall, long-legged lanky figure coming toward me. It was a clown on stilts. He must have been eight or nine feet tall. He had the face paint and the big shoes. He was getting closer and closer. At first, I was okay with that. I'd seen clowns before. I may have even yelled to him. He kept coming closer and closer—straight toward me, with his big creepy grin and his arms swinging. I stood there very nervous. Suddenly, without warning, he reached down and scooped me up. He tucked me under his arm and kept walking down the parade route as I dangled there, high in the air. I was looking down at the ground, and then back up at the smirking clown. And I started screaming, "Nuh-oooooooh!" I was terrified, utterly powerless to escape his clutch, and nobody seemed to understand how scared I was. Even today, it's an unpleasant memory. Along with the fear of cows and trees, I have a legitimate fear of clowns.

There are so many things that people are afraid of, and so many reasons why they fear. I'd like to add one more phobia to the list. Phobophobia. That is, of course, the fear of phobias. Franklin D. Roosevelt once said, "The only thing we have to fear is fear itself."

So rather than chase the clowns away, run from the spiders, or square off with the bananas, what we really have to do is face the FEAR. We can react in a couple of different ways.

When fear confronts us, most likely one of the following things will happen. We will: a) Freeze, b) Flee, or c) Fight.

When we FREEZE, we miss what's going on around us. Like a deer caught in the headlights of life, we can become so sidetracked, or immobilized by fear, that we don't hear God speaking to us. He is trying to lead us—to guide and direct us with His voice, but because we are so afraid of what's about to happen, we can't hear Him.

Further, we get blinders to the people around us who are hurting and in need of God's love and healing. We can't act because our fear paralyzes us.

It may be that God wants to use us to do something incredible; instead, we freeze and turn to stone, as in the following illustration from Matthew.

In Matthew 26:59-75 the disciple Peter was in the garden with Jesus, when soldiers showed up to arrest Jesus. At that moment, Peter's love for his teacher was so great that he was willing to die for Him. He pulled out a sword, and started chopping away, when Jesus said, "Hey, put away the sword—those who live by the sword will die by the sword," and He explained to Peter that this was all part of God's plan. Peter gave in, "All right," he said, while he reluctantly watched Jesus taken away. The next part of this scripture is very interesting; it says Peter followed from afar. He was afraid.

Once they reached the town, Peter had a chance to observe the ill treatment of his master, Jesus. So, when somebody came up to him and said, "Hey, aren't you one of his followers? You were with Jesus of Nazareth, right?" he had an opportunity to witness; the door was open for him to say, "Yeah, I WAS with Him. Let me tell you how amazing He is.

Let me tell you—He's God. Let me tell you what He did for me. I've watched him heal. I've watched him walk on water. I, myself, have walked on water because of Him. Let me tell you . . ." All these things, he could have said. But he let his fear speak instead. He froze up and said, "No. No, no, I don't know him. I don't know what you're talking about."

Before he had time to reflect on what he had done, a second person came up and said, "Hey, aren't you one of them?" "No. Not me. You must have me confused with someone else." For the second time he said, "No I don't know him."

Then, a little girl came up and said, "Hey, your accent—you sound like one of them. The way you talk—I know you've been with this man, Jesus." For the third time, Peter denied his relationship. He called down curses and said, "No! I do not know the man!"

How sad. Peter had just spent three years of his life with Jesus. He was a member of His inner circle. He LOVED Jesus; but fear made him follow from afar. He let fear control him. Whatever allowed him to get to the point where he felt compelled to say, "I don't know the man," had to be an extreme fear, indeed. Perhaps, he felt threatened by what Jesus' enemies might say—afraid his reputation would be ruined, or afraid he might be arrested. Worse yet, perhaps he feared that he was going to be killed. It is amazing what the emotion of fear will do to us—how it freezes us up.

I tell you this story in the hopes it will open your eyes and you will not let fear keep you from saying, "I DO know Him!" I see a lot of people—both teenagers and adults, who may not verbalize the statement, "I don't know the man," but may say it with their actions.

Because of fear we often find ourselves in groups that we know we shouldn't be in. Sometimes, Christians will say, "I don't know the man," by their lifestyles, through the things that they are doing (or not doing), or the choices that they are making. They say, "I don't know the man," by drinking what they shouldn't, just because their friends are doing so. Or they say, "I don't know the man," when they decide they're going to watch a certain movie, or go to a certain place to do this or that. Because their peers are watching, and they're afraid of being different, they seem to be unable to take a stand. They can't say, "I don't watch those kinds of movies. I can't listen to that song. I'm not going to that party, and I'm not going to smoke that with you, or drink that." So when they're around a certain group of people, they let fear immobilize them, and when they say nothing they are really saying, "I don't know the man."

Maybe, we don't freeze in the face of fear, but instead we have the inclination to FLEE. Fear can cause us to ignore our troubles.

In the book of Luke, Chapter 10, you can read about *The Good Samaritan*. It's a story that begins with a traveling man who was down and out; he was robbed, stripped of his clothing and valuables, then beaten and left lying in a crumpled heap on the side of the road.

He was barely alive when a "pastor" showed up, glanced down at the guy, and directly walked over to the other side of the road. Was it fear that drove him away? Maybe he thought, "I'll get beat up, if I stop to help; I might get caught in something I don't know how to deal with." Whatever his reasoning, he left the hurt man lying there, and walked over to the other side, as far away from him as he could get.

Then along came a "rich guy," a Levite, and he thought, "Man, I don't want to get involved in this!" Was it fear that also caused him to walk on the other side? I can't say for sure, but we are told that is what he did.

A Samaritan, however, was traveling the same road. When he came upon the man, he felt sorry for him. He jumped right in with bandages and ointment. He said, "I've got you… this is going to be okay." Then, he put his own coat on him, laid him on the back of his own donkey, and took him to a place where he could get some real help.

I think one of the greatest tools of the enemy is fear. Satan uses it to control God's people, knowing that ultimately God wants to use us. If the devil can strike us with fear, he will put a stop to this blessing. We miss God's voice, and we miss people who are hurting. Don't let fear make you deaf and blind to what's happening around you. There is no shortage of hurting people in this world, because it's a messed up, sinful place. God is still here to rescue. And he needs his people to do their part.

"Jesus says, "My grace is all you need. My power works best in weakness." So now I am glad to boast about my weaknesses, so that the power of Christ can work through me."
~ 2 Corinthians 12:9 (NLT)

Even if fear does not immobilize us or cause us to ignore issues, it may cause us to FLEE. We run away. Mark 4:35-40 tells a great story. Jesus and his followers were on the shores of a lake, where Jesus had been preaching. They were tired, and He said, "Let's go on over to the other side." So they all jumped into a boat together, and began to head across the water, looking forward to a little rest and relaxation. The day was fair when they began their voyage. However, storms can rise in a split second out of nowhere. Just so, out of the clear blue sky, a storm whipped up on the sea. One minute everything was going along great and in the next moment, they were in serious trouble.

Meanwhile, Jesus was completely exhausted. He had gone to the stern of the boat to take a nap. He was relaxed with his head on a cushion, completely oblivious to the squall. He wasn't worried about the boat capsizing or anything else. He was in a calm sleep, but his followers were getting extremely nervous. In fact, they were scared senseless, running around, terrified, acting crazy and yelling, "What are we supposed to do? We're all going to die!" Then they realized that Jesus was asleep. So they ran to him, woke him up, and demanded an explanation, "Jesus, don't you CARE if we drown? Don't you care about us at ALL?"

Do you know how many people have said that before? "Don't you care that I'm going through this storm? Don't you care that I have this hurt? Don't you care?"

I have said those same words. That was how I felt when my wife and I lost our first child. "God, don't you love me? Don't you care about me? Everything was fine in my life—we were all doing great here, when all of a sudden 'boom'—with a snap of the fingers, this baby doesn't make it. Hey, God, don't you love me?"

But, here is what Jesus said. First he calmed the storm—which would have been an amazing sight to see—and then He said the most awesome thing ever, "Hey. Where is your faith in me? Don't fear. I'm here." That is the main point for us to remember. Jesus is in the boat with us.

When we go through storms and have fear in our lives (which we will), if we know Jesus and have a relationship with him, then He is in our boat, and we are going to be okay.

The people that I'm most concerned about are those that are not in the boat. They're struggling, they're fighting to stay above the water, they're not in the boat, they're separated from Jesus, and so they're drowning. It happens every day.

When trouble comes, we may run TO God, or run AWAY from Him. Or we can stand and FIGHT.

We are accountable to fight the fear that threatens to control us. Only then can we bring those people in the boat with us. If we let fear govern us, we fail to hear the cries of others, we miss the opportunity to reach out to broken people, we miss the voice of God, and instead we are likely to run away from him.

Fear is always at hand. I'm not saying I am immune. I am confronted by fears all the time. I frequently wonder about the future, or what will happen if I choose to act a certain way. We don't have to give in to our fears.

One thing that has helped me to overcome, as I encounter all the different fears in my life, is a promise found in 2 Timothy 1:7-8. The scripture says that fear doesn't come from God. He says the spirit of love, the spirit of power, and the spirit of self-discipline are greater than fear. Self-discipline is sometimes translated as "a sound mind." It is a condition that we cannot create within ourselves. It's a gift, and it gives us peace.

Right after I "got saved" I remember telling my dad about the change in my life. He didn't know what I meant. I tried to explain it to him, but he didn't understand and he was irrational in his drunken, "messed up" condition. He was going to hurt me so I ran into the woods and he was chasing me, but I hid behind a tree. I'd just been saved the night before and had never really prayed in my life until then. At that moment, I began to pray. "God help me! I don't even know what that means. God, I don't even know you; I just met you, but help me!" That night, as I was hanging out behind that tree, I felt a sense of peace that God was with me there, and I did not have to be afraid.

Fear can move us in different ways, but we can't let fear crush us. When God is part of our life, we can defeat the fears. The spirit of power, spirit of love, and the spirit of a sound mind will overcome in us the fears we face in whatever "crash" we may be in.

It took me a few years to learn how to be a dad. I

honestly didn't have a good example of a dad in my own life, and I didn't always feel comfortable that I could be a good father. So when my wife suggested I spend time with our firstborn, Coleton, one on one, without her, I was more than a little nervous. I never really did anything with the boys without Vickie along, because I wasn't really sure how a Daddy was supposed to act. She would go do things with the kids without me, but I just didn't have the confidence to act like a father. I think I was afraid I'd forget them somewhere; I'm not really sure.

Anyway, it was late October, and she said to me, "Coleton wants to be a superhero for Halloween." He was three or four years old. "You know what? Take him to Toys R Us. Go buy him a costume; just remember to bring him back." I thought, "I can do that. I can remember to bring him back." So we got to the store and we walked in the door, and it was all decked out for Halloween. I said "Hey, Coleton, this is cool, right? We're gonna get a costume, and you can be a superhero!" He just stopped at the door, taking in all the scary-looking stuff with wide eyes. I tried to coax him along, and convince him that everything was okay. It was intimidating for such a little guy. I urged him to come on in, but he wouldn't budge. So I took his hand and led him along until we came up to a counter, with what appeared to be a severed head resting on it. I went over and grabbed the head up by the hair. I just wanted to show him that it wasn't real. "See, there's nothing to be afraid of here." I wanted to free him from his perceived fear by showing him there was no danger. I could tell by his face that he was thinking, "I don't believe you."

So, I held this ugly head up by the hair and I said, "Look! It's plastic. It's not real." I was joking around like that, when I saw a little sticker on the ear that said, "Press me." Without thinking, I reached in and squeezed the ear. Mistake. Big mistake. A creepy, deep Transylvanian voice uttered the spooky command, "Come closer!"

I was only slightly startled, because I was expecting something to happen. "Look Coleton! It's talking!" I laughed a little. Then I reassured him, "Look it's not real," because he was just standing there with the most petrified look on his face you've ever seen. The poor kid's eyes were bugged out and his expression said, "You're kidding me, right? You've got a head in your hand and it's talking! That's crazy!'

Unaware of what was about to happen, I walked closer to him saying, "Look, it's fine." The head simply repeated, "Come Close-uhr!" Then, out of nowhere, as I held the head up, trying to convince him it wasn't real, the jaw flew open, the tongue shot out of its mouth and hit him in the forehead, the eyeballs popped out, and it uttered a crazy scream, and now I was surprised. I hollered, "Braawwwhhhhhhhh…" I screamed, my kid screamed, and he tore off through Toys R Us as fast as he could run. As I watched the back of him speeding down the aisle away from me, I came to myself and realized, "I've lost him!"

Then I set off, chasing him through the toy store. In my rush and excitement to catch my son . . . I did not set the head down! Where was my brain? I don't know. I was chasing along behind my little boy, with an insane looking head in my hand, yelling at him. "Come here, Coleton. Don't run away." He looked back at me, saw the head in my hand, and with a horrified shriek, he ran even faster. Finally, I came to my senses, and threw the head down. He dove into a clothing rack, and I stood on the outside of it calling him, "Coleton, come to me. I'm so sorry. I didn't mean to scare you."

At this point, he looked through the parted clothes to see whether I still had the head in my hands. Again I said, "I'm sorry. I didn't know it was gonna do that." When he saw that it was safe, he darted out of the rack and jumped into my arms. I mean, he threw his arms around me, clung to me and cried, "Hold me, Daddy," and I sat there and held him.

It was me that caused fear to my son, but ultimately he knew he could run to me; he knew I would take care of him. He was confused at first, because I was the one holding that scary head. When he recognized I loved him and meant him no harm, he jumped into my arms, and I just held him there.

It was a great teachable moment for me also. This is an example of how a person responds when he is afraid in life. He might run away from God, but the best thing to do is to run TO Him. I realize that when I go through storms or fear in my own life, I should run to my Father. He's ready to wrap me in His strong, comforting arms, with the assurance, "I've got you, you're in my boat, and I'm not going to let you go!"

"There is no fear in love, but perfect love casts out fear."
~ 1 John 4:18 (NIV)

.

CHAPTER 5

The Voice

*"The gatekeeper opens the gate for him,
and the sheep listen to his voice.
He calls his own sheep by name and leads them out.
When he has brought out all his own, he goes on
ahead of them, and his sheep follow him
because they know his voice."*
~ *John 10:3-4 (NIV)*

As I was running back and forth through the woods, first looking for the pocketknife, next trying to locate help out in the open pasture, and then hurrying back to my grandparents at the plane crash, I kept getting lost.

There was, without a doubt, a trail of debris that would

61

lead me back to the initial crash site as long as I didn't lose track of that trail. But once I got beyond the trees and into the pasture, I was so intent on searching for help, while avoiding cows and other potential dangers, that I couldn't always find my way back to where the plane had entered the woods. I couldn't see where the line of wreckage started. So, I'd get down the tree line and begin to wonder what part of the pasture I was in. Had I walked to the other side of it without realizing it, or was I in the same place I started? It was just a big square to me, and I wasn't even sure which corner I was on. And then, there were the cows—I was so distracted by them—and so, much of the time I was totally disoriented.

I would walk over to the place where I thought I should be, and I'd be very still and quiet, and I would listen. Sooner or later, I would hear my grandma's voice way off in the distance through the trees. "Kacy!" She would call my name and I would jump over the fence and walk a little bit and stop. Then I'd hear the call. "Ka-acy ...," so I would revive and walk in that direction once more. Then I'd stop again and lean against a tree. If I didn't hear anything for a long time, I'd just rest and wait. The heat was so exhausting. There were times that I actually passed out and woke again only after I heard Grandma call.

I would hear that voice, and I immediately recognized it. It was very familiar to me. It was my grandma. It was the grandmother that that had always cared for me and made visits to her house so special, the grandmother who loved me and wanted to protect me from danger, the grandmother who was in the plane yelling for me to put my head down, the grandmother that was so amazing that even at this dreadful hour, with her life hanging in the balance, she was concerned for my safety.

That was how I knew how to get back to the crash site. I would listen, and I knew that voice like no other voice. When I heard her call my name, I would get my bearings and follow the sound. I'd get to the next tree and the next tree after that, and I'd get to a place that looked somewhat familiar and I'd finally find my way back to the plane site.

Oddly, I felt more comfortable there, even though my grandpa had already passed away. I suppose it was because my grandma was there. She couldn't move; she was in great pain and neither of us knew what was going to happen. It seemed as though she was slipping away. Yet as long as I could hear her voice, it was an anchor that brought me back to where I felt safe.

As we struggle through life, I often wonder whose voice we are listening to? Is it the right voice? There are so many different voices that we hear in this world, but only one voice to which we should really give our attention.

There is power in a voice. That became a reality to me when my first son Coleton was born. As I've said, Vickie and I had already gone through a miscarriage. We suffered through the pain of losing of our first child and then we learned that we were pregnant again. We were going to have a baby, but things were a little different now. At least, at this point we were praying for God's will and believing that whatever was meant to be would be. I won't deny we dealt with a little fear. We wondered if we were ready to go through this again. We learned that the only way to overcome our anxieties was to pray every night and give it all over to God. We had to trust Him and then believe that everything was going to be fine and good.

The term was going well. The baby was growing. We went for an ultrasound, and listened to the heart beating a strong "Dit-dit-dit-dit! Everything was developing properly and it was great to trust that God was really in charge of this pregnancy. Vickie and I rested in the confidence that an all-knowing God was in charge of the details of our family and our future.

We left the past in the past, and on May 20th, 2002, showed up at the hospital with high hopes, looking forward to having this "fun little addition." We expected everything to be okay this time around, and that we would make it through the delivery just fine and everyone would live happily ever after.

A couple of hours ticked by, and it was almost boring. There were a lot of devices hooked up to Vickie. On one monitor we could hear her heartbeat, and the baby's was on another that they had attached to her stomach. We could hear the beeping. It was a very regular, but rapid "Bipp-bipp-bipp-bipp-bipp." My kid's heartbeat was going 90 mph, it seemed, and it was all just fine.

Then the labor kicked in—NOT so boring anymore!!! The scene changed instantly from a nice room, with television, family members, cozy curtains and relaxed atmosphere to… "Okay, everybody out!"

We had done Lamaze classes (a fun little time together in our life), so naturally I thought, "I'm going to do what I have learned now." I was ready to coach. She was in position, leaning back just like in class. She was trying to breathe and that was just what we had trained for. I had gone to all the classes. I had gotten a certificate, and I was prepared for this. So I leaned over her, shouting "C'mon! Baby, you got this!" I didn't even know what I was saying. But she started hissing, "sh-sh-shh," while I cheered, "Yeah, yeah... breathe!" ... And she repeated ... "Sh-sh-sh-sh-sh ... sh-sh-sh!" Again I cheered, "Yeah, come on!" I then kind of hissed back at her. Finally, she put her hand up, and put it on my face. No! She actually grabbed my face and said, "Noooo! SHHH... Shhh... SHUT UP! Get out of my face, you're sucking all my air!" And since I can take a subtle hint, I stepped aside. My coaching was done and I renounced my post with a simple, "Oh, sorry . . . Yeah, I'm gonna be right over here, if you need me." After that, I silently applauded her efforts from a safe distance.

This seemed to go on forever; she actually went through 16 hours of weary labor—agonizing down to the last hour. Then suddenly things started getting really weird. She had spent all this time in labor and he still wasn't coming out—she wasn't dilating—nothing was happening!

All along I had been hearing this heartbeat going at a fast "beepeepeep"... and suddenly it began to slow down. The nurses ran to put an oxygen mask on my wife. Her mother had been with us in the room and an attendant told her, "Ma'am, you have to leave." My wife then turned her head toward me and our eyes met across the space and in my mind I yelled, "Oh, no! Here we go again! We've been HERE before!!!" I realized however, that I had to let go and say, "Okay, God. You're in control of this. I'm listening for you at this moment." As I began to calm down, abruptly the heartbeat changed from " Bipbipbipbipbip" to a screeching halt "beeeeeeeeeee." It flat lined.

I've seen enough movies, and hospital-type shows on TV to know that one constant beep is NOT good. So, I was standing frozen with my mouth and eyes wide open, freaking out inside. This woman, the nurse, grabbed my wife's belly and began to shake it. I watched her in silent fear, disbelief registered in my mind, "Hey, she's shaking my wife's belly... what are we doing here?"

And while I stood concerned, she looked up and pointed at me and said, "Daddy!" Daddy. I hadn't ever been called that before. I didn't even know what that meant. Are you kidding me? Did she just call ME daddy? In fact, when she first called "Daddy," I figured she must have been talking to HER daddy, and I thought, "That's weird; this woman's dad is in the room. Why is HE here? And why does she need him right now?" So I started to turn around to say, "Hey, your daughter needs you," when I realized she meant ME.

She looked straight at me and yelled, "YOU, YOU!!" I pointed at my chest and whispered, "Me?" "Ye-es! You!" And I'll never forget what she said next. "Let him hear your voice." So I walked over and cupped my hand to my mouth over Vickie's stomach and called his name. I said "Coleton!" Come out of there." It's all I could think to say. "Get out of there. I want to meet you. We love you. We want to see you." And in that instant, "Bam!" The silent monitor resumed "Beeeep-beeep-beep-bip-bip-bip-bip-bip." It started to speed up again! I was thinking, "Are you freaking kidding me?" The doctor seemed just as amazed. He looked over at the screen, and then he looked at me and said "Wuh-hut?!" Even though we were all dumbfounded, he took command again. "This baby has got to come out right now!" Instantly they all disappeared with a "whoosh"… Every single person, except for me, rushed from the room.

They were all gone; and as they left me I'm standing in awe, thinking, "Did that just happen?" I was totally flustered. My wife was gone. I was by myself completely, and I just stood there in this suddenly empty room and, in the quietness, I HEARD A VOICE. "It's ok. I've got you. I'm going to take care of you." I just remember a peaceful feeling washed over me, a quiet joy filled me and I knew: God has got this! I didn't hear an audible voice announcing, "Kacy!" over a loudspeaker, or anything like that... But He spoke to me in a still, small voice in the midst of my personal storm, and peace came to me instantly.

And then someone official came in and gave me a bunch of special stuff to put on. They had taken Vickie to an operating room to do an emergency Caesarean Section. They told me to come so I followed them into this room, and immediately ran and sat down next to my wife. I wanted to reassure her. I said, "It's okay," and she said, "I know. We're good." What I didn't know at the time was Vickie had heard the same voice telling her everything was going to be ok. God had given her the same peace He had given me.

I could hear all the sounds going on around me—the doctor's abrupt orders, the suction noise, machines going "ding, ding, ding"... But it was all just background as I waited. Then to my surprise, the doctor looked at me and asked, "Hey, do you want to look at this? And I said, "Hey, do you want to pick me up off the floor?

Because that's what you will be doing… I'm gonna stay on this end if you don't mind!" He chuckled. "OK. I was just giving you the option." I said, "Here's a camera, take some pictures, and I'll look at them later."

Then I heard the doctor from the other end. "Here's the problem. The cord is wrapped around his neck." He removed it, and they pulled him out. I saw some tiny little feet pass my face, as the doctor handed him to this other guy who took him over to a table. We knew something was not right. We had been watching the baby channel for the last nine months, and we knew the first thing that happens when a baby comes out is they cry. We heard nothing. At that time my son was still not breathing—there was nothing coming out. My wife asked, "Why is he not crying?" I said, "I don't know, but he's okay; I know he's okay."

It seemed an eternity as I watched this man with a little bag, pushing on the baby's stomach and doing other stuff, but all I could see of Coleton were his tiny feet. I don't know how many minutes went by. And then I heard a shrill "Wahhhh!" from across the room, and I was overjoyed. I turned to celebrate with Vickie. "High Five! Oh, we can't . . . you're strapped down!"

We heard a wail like a siren and a thrill of joy flooded

our hearts. We had a great sense of relief. I was thankful that I heard God's voice and that it had given me peace.

John Chapter 10, Verse 2 says this: "He who enters in by the gate is the shepherd of the sheep. The gatekeeper opens the gate for Him, and the sheep listen to his voice.

He calls his own sheep by name and leads them out. When He has brought out all his own, He goes on ahead of them, and His sheep follow him because they know his voice."

It stands to reason that if we spend time with God, we will understand his voice. But when we spend time with the world, or away from God, we're not going to be able to recognize His voice when he speaks to us.

John Chapter 10, Verse 5 says, "they will never follow a stranger, in fact they will run away from him because they do not recognize a strangers voice."

It's possible that we can spend so much time in this world that the voice of the world becomes more familiar to us. Where does that voice come from? Whose voice is it?

Genesis Chapter 3 tells us the story of the fall of man. God created Adam and Eve, placed them in the Garden of Eden, and gave them everything they needed to live. They had no pain, no shame, no fear, and all was good. Man was created in God's image and likeness, which means we are not robots, but have free will. So, God put the Tree of Knowledge of Good and Evil in the middle of the garden and instructed Adam and Eve not to touch it. He told them they could eat from any other tree in the garden, but not to touch that one. He did this to give them an opportunity to make a true moral choice.

> *Now the serpent was more crafty than any of the wild animals the Lord God had made.*
>
> *He said to the woman, "Did God really say, 'You must not eat from any tree in the garden'?"*
>
> *The woman said to the serpent, "We may eat fruit from the trees in the garden, but God did say, 'You must not eat fruit from the tree that is in the middle of the garden, and you must not touch it, or you will die.'"*
>
> *"You will not certainly die," the serpent said*

*to the woman. "For God knows that when
you eat from it your eyes will be opened, and
you will be like God, knowing good and
evil."*

*When the woman saw that the fruit of the
tree was good for food and pleasing to the
eye, and also desirable for gaining wisdom,
she took some and ate it.*

*She also gave some to her husband, who was
with her, and he ate it.*
                                      ~ *Genesis 3:1-6 (NIV)*

Something that really jumps out at me about this
passage is that Adam and Eve found themselves right
next to the one thing they were not supposed to
touch. They were right next to that tree they were
told specifically to stay away from. Before they realized
it, they were listening to a voice that was questioning
whether God really said they weren't supposed to touch
it. Isn't it ironic how we so often find ourselves in the
middle of something we know we shouldn't be in the
middle of? Before we realize it, we are listening to
that same voice Adam and Eve heard, asking us if God
really said we shouldn't be doing whatever it is we are
doing. This is why it is so important to know the

voice of God, through reading His word. Then, when we are faced with those situations or circumstances, we are able to keep from falling into temptation.

In Vickie's book, *For Him – Guidance for Christian Athletes,* she shares her story about listening to the wrong voice. She listened to a voice that told her she wasn't good enough, pretty enough, thin enough, etc. Vickie fell into the lies that led her to a 12 year struggle with anorexia and bulimia. There is a passage of scripture that became solid for Vickie to hold onto through recovery. It is still one that she leans on today.

> *I will walk about in freedom, for I have sought out your precepts.   ~ Psalm 119:45 (NIV)*

Vickie saw her struggle as a prison, and the voice that was lying to her would not go away. The word precept also means principle, commandment, or doctrine. This verse taught her that if she would seek after God's word, He would lead her to freedom.

The freedom that she has experienced ultimately comes through the victory Jesus endured on the cross. The same opportunity God gave Adam and Eve to choose, He also gives us. Ultimately it is our choice to decide which voice we will listen to and follow.

CHAPTER 6

ALONE

"Cast all your anxiety on Him,
because He cares for you."
~ 1 Peter 5:7 (NIV)

As long as I could hear my grandma's voice, I had a sense that I was not all by myself in this crazy mess. But, unfortunately, the tragedy was real. My grandpa was dead, and my grandma was in and out of consciousness. When I comprehended that she might die too, I began to understand that I was alone, and it scared me. I did not like that feeling at all.

I was scared. I had no idea if we would ever be rescued, but I knew that if help were around, it would be up to me to find it. So I once again headed out toward the unknown. Alone. When I could no longer hear my grandma speaking, everything in my world seemed to stand still. In the noiseless confusion, nothing made sense. I felt as if I was wading through a bad dream—in silence and slow motion. I wandered aimlessly looking for help—from where, I did not know.

Looking back, I don't really know how much time I spent alone. I don't know the actual timeframe in which everything happened, but to a small child it seemed like absolutely forever. The loneliness was intensified by the realization that my grandpa was dead, my grandma was on her way out, and I was, in a practical sense, all by myself. I didn't know whether I would be rescued or end up spending the night alone, or if I was going to die myself. I didn't know what to do. At that time, I was not aware of the Biblical principal found in Genesis 2:18: *"It is not good that man should be alone."* However, I deeply felt the reality of that truth.

I was giving my best effort—looking for help—and getting lost over and over. I couldn't see or hear another human being. Apparently, even the cows were taking a break. Gazing over the pasture, one of the things I remember was how silent it was. In my memory, I can hear the breeze blowing through the trees—and

wind would stop and it would get so still and so quiet…
Yes, it was very lonely.

> *"Be still and know that I am God."*
> *~ Psalm 46:10 (NIV)*

As a child, this loneliness was a rare, unknown feeling.
A few years down the road, however, I became familiar
with solitude. I was in my adolescent years when I
went to live with my Dad.

Up to this time, I had lived with my brother and
mother. My father was not part of the scene. When I
was in 7th grade, I started getting into a lot of trouble at
school. There had been a great deal of anger building
inside me. I was angry with my mother. I was angry
at my life circumstances. I was just plain mad at life. I
should not have blamed my mom; she did an amazing
job raising two kids alone. She had no help at all—no
support from my father; she was sometimes working
two jobs, and doing everything in her power to take
care of us two boys. And I wasn't the easiest kid to get
along with, because I had a lot of rage and resentment.
I blamed the situation on her, I blamed my dad, I was
mad at the world, and I kept having little problems rise
up here and there.

the creaking sounds in the tops of the pines. Then the Whenever I would have a little trouble, I'd get defiant and throw the idea out there, "Oh yeah? I'll just go and live with my dad!" I'm sure many people can relate to that attitude. Although I was also very angry with my dad, that seemed to be my last hope. Sure. I was mad at him, but I also craved his affection. This is very difficult to explain and hard to comprehend unless you have been in this situation yourself. I was angry with the man I felt was to blame for my unhappiness, but I still longed for his affection and approval; I wanted him to like me. I wanted him to LOVE me. I wanted him to play ball with me and just be a father. I wanted those things, but couldn't get them. So, I reached out in desperation to see if he would reach back.

Anyway, day after day, I was getting into trouble with my mom, so I thought I could go live with my dad and maybe things would be easier (knowing in my heart that they probably wouldn't). My mom said, "This is a very bad idea." But, she let me do it anyway. We located my dad in a place called Benton, Louisiana. I had no clue where that was, but that's where he was living when I called and asked if I could come live with him. He reluctantly said, "Yes," and took me in.

Unfortunately, that move was like waking up from one

nightmare to be caught in another. I left my troubled life in Galveston, where I had been getting into a little bit of difficulty now and then, and went walking into this crazy life with a Dad who was an alcoholic and didn't really care about me.

I went to live with him, and immediately discovered there was a lot of weird stuff going on in his life. He'd take me to bars, parties, and things like that—places a young teenager did not belong. But worse than that, he would always leave me places: He would leave me alone in bars; he would leave me alone in peoples' homes; he would leave me alone at school.

A lot of the time, rather than leave me home alone, he would take me with him when he went out. We would frequently end up in bars or in his friends' homes, and he would get busy drinking alcohol and ignore me. I would sit at the bar with a glass of Sprite and a bowl of cherries, while he got so drunk that he forgot that I was with him. So he would walk out and leave me, sometimes at 2:00 in the morning. Occasionally, he'd go off to somebody else's house and pass out and wake up the next day, and frequently, even from those places he would go home without a single thought about me. At these times, I felt totally abandoned.

Every now and then, waitresses or bartenders would give me a ride. I did live pretty far out in the woods though, so I didn't get those offers very often. If I had no other way, then I had to walk down some deserted country roads to get myself back home. Or I would go sleep in a stairwell somewhere—just anywhere I could find some safety and seclusion until daylight. Sometimes, I'd even walk over to the school and hang out there.

After I'd made a couple of friends in Benton, on a few occasions I would go to one of their houses. I would knock on the glass, and if they would take me, I'd crawl through the window and sleep at their house. I'd do that whenever I got a chance.

At other times, my dad would actually leave me at home for several days and take off for places unknown. One of the most desolate moments was when he was away on a drinking binge over the weekend. He was absent for two or three days. I got off the bus from school and went inside the house to find that the electricity had been cut off. Then I really felt what it was like to be alone!

I had no food, no electricity, and no companionship. I had to spend Friday, Saturday, and Sunday completely by myself, in complete darkness with hardly a bite to eat, nothing going on, and no one around. It was really tough. I spent a lot of time outside and went inside at night, to light a candle and go to sleep, hoping that my dad would show up. Sometimes I hoped he wouldn't show up, because I knew he would be drunk and out of control. That lonesome weekend finally came to an end. Then, I had to go to school on Monday. But I spent many weekends on my own, like this. True loneliness was really sinking into my life.

I think the worst times of all were when he would forget to pick me up from school. There would be teachers passing by me on their way home. The custodians would finish their work and leave. And I would be the last one at the school, all by myself, just hoping that maybe my father would remember to come get me. Back then, people didn't really check on you— they didn't stop and ask, "Hey, do you have a ride? Is someone coming to get you?" They would just tend to their business and leave.

And when they were all gone, it would get dark and I would just sit there waiting. Finally, I would give up; I would find a little place to lay down and I'd spend the night there in the school. It was not very comfortable. I didn't sleep very well. Those were not great nights.

In the morning, I'd get up and go to class. This was emotionally challenging. I had missed dinner and breakfast, which was in itself difficult, but then I had to show up in class wearing the same clothes I was wearing the day before. I was hungry, dirty and embarrassed. The other kids would make fun of me; they'd pick on me or have nothing to do with me.

Early on, I spent a lot of time at the school, not really knowing a lot of people. Being new to a school is always tough. But, I encountered a lot of lonesomeness in those hallways. Nobody wanted to speak to me or spend time with me at first. Eventually, I did make some friends—at least, I met some people who would talk to me.

Because of the type of ministry I am in, I encounter a lot of teenagers, and even adults, that spend massive amounts of time alone. I've seen young people, who should be enjoying their youthful years, experiencing loneliness, depression, and even contemplating suicide instead. This is because they spend so much time alone, unaware that there is a way to overcome loneliness. My desire for you, as you're reading this book and learning about my story, is to know that you are NOT alone!

I go to a lot of high schools and middle schools to

speak, and one of the things that I always notice at these places are students sitting by themselves at lunchtime, and sitting alone in hallways. When I see them, it takes me back. My past reaches out to me, when I look into these students' eyes and wonder what sort of hurt is taking place behind the lonely faces. I was that kid. I remember what it felt like to be lonesome—to not have a friend to enjoy lunch with—not a soul to talk to, to share what was happening in my life. There was no one who cared that I was going to an empty home and an unpredictable dad. I never knew from one day to the next if I was going to be facing an intoxicated jerk, or if I'd be left alone for another three days by an invisible father.

One time I saw a little girl sitting all alone. I had spoken at the school earlier that day, and so the students knew me. I was hanging out at the school that afternoon when I noticed her sitting near a wall, by herself, and I felt the urge to just go say, "Hi,"—nothing more than a quick "Hey, how are ya? Hope you enjoyed the talk today."

As I walked up to her, she recognized that I was the guy that had made her laugh at the presentation earlier, and tears welled up in her eyes. I was a little startled. I looked down at her and said, "Hey, are you okay? She looked right back in my face and said, "No. No, I'm not. I go home to your story every day. I go home not knowing if my dad is going to be there or not. I have no friends at this school; I get picked on. I get bullied. I have nobody."

I hear these stories every time I go to a school! It's going on more than you may think in this world right now.

Since it's at a school, I am not supposed to share Jesus with them. But, I can make an effort to reassure them that things are going to be okay. There is a cure for loneliness. I try to encourage students to get involved with youth groups—to get involved with different church programs. Our church has Life Groups; we urge people to get involved in these groups. They give people an opportunity to meet and fellowship with others that may have similar struggles and life issues and understand the stuff that they're going through. They can come together in these core groups and establish friendships and enjoy positive interaction. It is helpful to be surrounded by likeminded people that can relate to you and your circumstances. So, I encourage students, teenagers and even adults to find your group. Find those with common interests. Find a group of people that you can enjoy hanging out with.

People are lonely for so many different reasons. They may have problems at home that they are ashamed about. They could be suffering from low self-esteem, or insecurities. They might experience depression from social or financial issues. Maybe they just want to hide from the world. You name it. It's out there. People are lonely. But, how do we overcome it? Jesus has promised to be our friend and we will never be lonely again. Jesus saw that we were worth something and He died to save us from our sins and from our despair. He gives us a sense of purpose and a joy in living that surpasses everything else.

> *"For you created my inmost being; you knit me together in my mother's womb. I praise you because I am fearfully and wonderfully made; your works are wonderful, I know that full well. My frame was not hidden from you when I was made in the secret place, when I was woven together in the depths of the earth. Your eyes saw my unformed body; all the days ordained for me were written in your book before one of them came to be."*
> *~ Psalm 139:13—16 (NIV)*

What should a person do to reach out when they see someone alone and friendless? How do they present Jesus? I talk to students all the time and I try to encourage them to reach out and do those things that I cannot do in a school setting.

I stand up and speak in front of groups of students. But, I can't reach them one on one like their classmates can. I can't be the creepy old man going around to all these kids who are sitting by themselves, doing nothing, and say "Hi." I really encourage people who are in the position to do so, to reach out. It's easy. They're a teenager; you're a teenager. You already have something in common. (If you're an adult, go to adults.)

It really amounts to just walking up and introducing yourself and saying, "Hello." If I see somebody sitting somewhere by themselves in the appropriate social situation, I will walk over and smile and say, "Hi... I'm Kacy, what's your name?" That's all. People are sometimes standoffish. Sometimes they're not. But, you never know what kind of impact you will have just by saying, "Hello." I hear story after story after story that confirms this.

A young lady who did not have a whole lot of friends at school was invited by a classmate to come to our *Disciple Now* youth retreat. At the retreat, she enjoyed the Bible studies and gave her life to Jesus; she is now plugged into our church. When she came to know

Jesus, she went back home to her family and they began to notice that she was different. They asked, "Hey, what's going on? And she responded, "Well, you've got to come to this church with me." They said, "Oh, no... we don't do church." But she was persistent. She just kept insisting, "You've got to come with me." Finally, her parents agreed. "Well, YOU are different; you're changing. I don't know what that is, but, sure... we'll go." So they showed up at church with her and met some believers, and decided, "Wow. This is different—this is not what we thought it was going to be." Very soon they were coming every Sunday. Now they're plugged into life groups, they're plugged into missions, they are involved with people, they're reading their Bibles and their lives have been changed. All this happened because one little girl was a missionary to her family.

It's crazy how often I see that happen—one person invites another: "Hey, how 'bout you come to church with me?" It's amazing to see the chain of events. In fact, that is how I got "saved." One kid invited me to church. (I'll tell that whole story a little later.)

But, here's another life changing story. I was speaking at a women's prison and numerous ladies came to Jesus at that time. It was one of the craziest things that I've ever been a part of in my life …

In the presentation, I had asked questions like: "Do you lie in bed at night and ask yourself, 'How did I get here?' 'What choices did I make that put me here?'" These women were in prison for a variety of reasons. Some were getting out soon, others in a few months or years, and some were never going to get out. It seemed that there was so much loneliness in the room. I was able to give the gospel and share an invitation for salvation. Over a hundred women prayed to receive Christ that day.

When I had finished, the women lined up to leave. I was gathering my stuff from against the wall when one woman broke from the line, to come over and talk to me. Wasting no time, she told me that she is never going to get out of prison, but today she "found freedom." I was moved by her testimony and I wanted to give her a hug, but we were in a high security setting and forbidden to touch these women at all. So I just asked her, "Ma'am, when is the last time you've had a hug?" She said, "I don't think I EVER remember having one." I said, "Well, I want to give you a hug, but it's against the rules. I can't touch you—I'm not allowed to hug you. But I want to give you a "wireless" hug." She looked at me kind of strangely and indicated she didn't understand what I meant.

And I repeated, "I want to give you a wireless hug. I'm going to hold my arms out, and you hold your arms out... and I'm just going to pretend like I'm hugging you, and you pretend like you're hugging me." And she said, "Okay." So, I stuck my arms out and she stuck her arms out, and I gave her a little "not touching" hug, and I told her, "Listen... I just want to let you know this. You are NEVER going to be alone again. You accepted Jesus into your life today, and He is never going to leave you. He's never going to forsake you. And you'll never be alone again. He's with you." She looked at me with tears pouring down her face, and said, "I believe you. I know that!"

It was a remarkable moment when I met this woman in prison, who had made some big mistakes in her life, but had found Jesus. It was the coolest thing to hear her say, "You know what? I know I'm never going to be alone again in this cell."

> *"Be strong and courageous. Do not be afraid or terrified because of them, for the Lord your God goes with you; he will never leave you nor forsake you."*
>
> ~ *Deuteronomy 31:6 (NIV)*

It is so lonely in prison and she could have chosen to just sit in that cell, and stare at the walls. But she had the assurance that she would never have to be alone again. She found a true companion in Jesus Christ.

If you accept Jesus into your life, He is with you. Jesus died for you and for each one of us. There is nothing we can do to earn salvation from Him. It's a gift from the One who sees each of us as so valuable that He gave his life and hung on a cross facing certain death.

THE loneliest moment ever (in all eternity) for Jesus had to be when His Father turned his face away while he was nailed to that cross. I don't think we can ever understand how he felt during that lonely moment described in Matt 27:46. Jesus cried out in a loud voice, "Eloi, Eloi, Lama Sabachthani?" (which means "My God, my God, why have you forsaken me?")

When Jesus was up there on that cross his disciples scattered, no one was there to comfort Him, even God had gone from him. It had to be a very lonely time. Even though he could have called it off at any moment, He endured it anyway. He had each of us in mind. He tasted death for us, so that we could live. And he went through all this, so we never have to be alone. He loves us and promises to be with each of us. He is offering us His friendship for eternity!

CHAPTER 7

The Fence

"I am the true vine, and my father is the gardener,
he cuts off every branch in me that bears no fruit,
while every branch that does bear fruit, he prunes…
so that it will be even more fruitful…
~ John 15: 1-2 (NIV)

Loneliness was not the only unfamiliar thing that I had to face in the crash. At 6 years old, I had never, ever seen a barbed wire fence, much less had to figure out how to get over one. But now, as I stood looking out into the pasture from the other side of an intimidating fence, I knew my survival was at stake if I didn't get past this obstacle.

When the plane hit the ground, we had bounced over

91

the fence and gone a couple hundred yards beyond it into the woods. So for me to get out into the field (or pasture, as they call it in East Texas), to find help, I had to get on the other side of this thing called "the barbed wire fence." As you can imagine, it was anything but easy.

First, since I didn't know any better, I just grabbed at it and of course my hands got all cut up. I tried crawling under it. It tore up my back. I tried going through the middle of it—between the wires—and it scratched my stomach. I tried to climb over it, but it slashed my legs and my hands. I was in and out—over and over—attempting to maneuver through it as the day wore on, because there was no way I was going to find help if I did not get past the barbed wire fence.

In much the same way that I had to face this painful hurdle, there are obstacles in life that each of us face as we struggle to make progress. There are serious things in life that we have to go through, or get past, and sometimes these hurt. Most of the time, they hurt a lot. But in order for us to get where we want to go, we must overcome the obstacles, whatever they may be.

If I couldn't get past the barbed wire, we would not be rescued—we weren't going to find help. If I didn't get through, we were going to die. Literally, there was no way we could have survived without getting help as soon as possible. My grandpa had already passed away. My grandma was hanging on and I knew I needed to find help, but it seemed the odds were against me.

It was bad enough that I felt smothered by the humid afternoon heat. And that dreadful barbed wire fence blocked my way to the pasture. Once I managed to get past the fence and out into the pasture, I had to be on guard against the cows. So, I had all these hurdles in my way, and I had to maneuver through them to find help. So I kept trying.

I don't know what you are facing today, but I know we all face difficulties regularly. The important question is, "What do we do to overcome our problems?"

Obstacles are inevitable. They can be an annoyance or they can <u>really</u> hurt, but they are often necessary for our growth. In the end, the pain we encounter may be just what we need to help us get where we should be, or to achieve the goals we have set. Or, it could be something even more than that. Keep in mind, as you struggle through difficulties, that this pain is not necessarily punishment or permanent.

When I was about 25 years old, I moved from the

Galveston area to Austin, Texas. I had been bouncing around from job to job, and I felt that I needed a fresh start. I needed something different—a new adventure in my life. After trying a few other jobs, I found one at a pawnshop. In the course of my work there, I saw some wild things. I could tell you story after story of what people brought in to pawn. The stuff was unreal—anything from cans of insect repellant to used toothpaste. You name it; people would bring it in asking, "Hey, how much can we get for this?" They were desperate for money…to spend on equally desperate causes. While it was a crazy place to work, I was a hard worker and moved up from a regular employee, to a higher-end employee, and finally I became an assistant manager at one of the company's stores.

Even though I was personally successful, my store was not in a very good part of town. True to their nature, pawnshops are not normally located in the best areas. As you can imagine, I was not working with positive influential people. There were drug dealers and prostitutes on the streets, not to mention the folks coming into the store, pawning junk. But, I *was* making really good money.

I was also performing stand-up comedy routines at I didn't have any other job planned, but I trusted their local clubs, bouncing around from one spot to another. I was doing well, keeping up with my bills, and had money in my pockets.

The summer before, I had met a couple named Steve and Rhonda Stoppe. They led the youth group for a church in the Austin area. As I was working my way up at the pawnshop job, they began to take me under their wings. I became a part of their youth ministry each week as they mentored me. At this time in my life, I was not even considering being in the ministry full-time, but they took a special interest in me and poured themselves into my life. They began asking questions about where I lived and worked, and other things like that. So I told them about my jobs.

At one point, some teenagers from the church actually came over to one of the comedy clubs where I was working, to watch me perform. Afterwards, I stood there while they watched the next act - and I became really convicted. My act wasn't dirty or anything like that, but some of the other routines were rather raunchy. I was struck by the fact that these students followed me into that club and, because of my influence, were seeing things that were not so great. I was more than a little bit concerned and ashamed about this.

advice. They said, "You need to quit that job." So, I said, "Okay." They were my mentors, and they were telling me that this was what I needed to do. And, the Lord had truly convicted me about the comedy club incident. I knew that my being in the environment where I lived and worked was not uplifting, nurturing, or good for my spiritual growth. So, I made the decision to quit and I didn't wait. I just walked in and I told my boss, "I'm quitting. I can't work here anymore." His response still makes me laugh when I think of it today. He said, "Oh yeah, well you can never work here again." I said, "Right! That's the whole point of my leaving. I'm NOT working here anymore."

So I quit, just like that, and for a little while it was okay. But, then I realized I was running out of money. I had to move out of the apartment where I was living, and then my car got repossessed. Suddenly, I was homeless; I had nowhere to stay—not even my car, since the bank took it back.

I had met a young worship guy at church, who was just a year or two out of high school and he understood my situation. He invited me to come and stay with him. He knew I had quit my jobs, and knew I didn't have any money, car or home. He had compassion and allowed me to move in with him.

He lived in a travel trailer—a small camper. It had bunk beds, but not much more, and I got to sleep on the couch. Basically my head was propped in the sink and my feet were literally hanging out the window. It was summertime, and it was super hot. But, humble as it was, it was shelter, and he was gracious enough to offer me a place to stay.

Meanwhile, I was really struggling to understand how I'd gotten to this point. I had money. I had a job. I had all the things I thought I needed in life. And I listened to what these people said, and took their advice. I honestly believed that God led me to do it but all of a sudden it seemed that everything was falling apart. It was crazy; everything was gone. I lost everything I had. At night I would lay on the couch (I wouldn't lay on the bed; I would lay on the couch...) and question God, "Hey, what's going on here? I don't understand. I'm doing what You asked me to do. And I'm going through this hardship—things are falling apart."

As far as I could tell, everything was NOT working out. I didn't understand it. It seemed that God had abandoned me, and it hurt. But here I was, night after night, having conversations with this young man who had opened his home to me. We would hang out and talk about spiritual things. He wanted to be a worship leader, and I would read my Bible and share things with him. We would talk about God and I would encourage him along his path.

So, on the one hand I was asking God, "Why are you doing this? Why is this happening?" But, on the other hand, I was telling this kid about Christ and how to follow Him. It was a crazy, conflicting time.

Eventually, I ended up moving out of his place and moving in with the Stoppes. They invited me to live with them while I was trying to get back on my feet. Rhonda is now a speaker and author. In her book, *"Moms Raising Sons to be Men,"* (Harvest House) she tells the story of my time with them:

> Kacy was in his twenties when we met him. *Hysterical* is the word I used at first to describe Kacy—one laugh after another. Yet as we came to know of the painful upbringing he had endured, *conflicted* was really a more accurate description.
>
> Kacy had accepted Christ when he was in eighth grade while living with his abusive, alcoholic father. Although Kacy had professed faith in Christ, he rebelled against God during his teenage years.

Early on Kacy found humor was a way to escape the pain of his home life. Working as a comedian in nightclubs, he found a place where he felt accepted and accomplished.

God developed an instant relationship between our family and Kacy. Week after week he came to our house for Bible study. Gradually the Lord transformed Kacy's thinking through His word. God's Spirit began to convict Kacy about the life he had chosen to pursue.

We did not have to impose legalism upon Kacy or beat him over the head with our Bibles to get him to see his talent was being wasted upon sinful pleasures. Teaching Kacy from God's word peeled back the calluses over Kacy's heart, caused him to repent, and stirred within him a desire to serve the Lord.

Eventually Kacy resigned from his nightclub work and moved in with our family. The Lord used this season to mature his walk with Christ. Feasting upon God's Word made an obvious change in Kacy's thinking. His perspectives on life began to be filtered through what he was learning from the Bible. Daily, Kacy discovered how to apply Scripture to his life. This, in turn, cultivated a new passion for God in his heart.

Joyfully, we saw this new foundation in God's truth

help Kacy work through painful memories from his childhood. He learned what God's Word said about forgiveness. Over time, Kacy was able to forgive the people who hurt him when he was a child. Soon our student became the teacher. Kacy showed an ability to teach from God's Word, and joined us in working with the youth at church. He zealously offered to others what had personally transformed his mind, heart, and life.

It soon became apparent that other teens identified with the struggles Kacy had experienced as a young man. His story offered hope to people living in what they thought were hopeless situations. When Kacy shared the gospel, kids came to Christ.

The Lord glorified Himself through the painful childhood Kacy had endured. Experiences that could have destroyed him became instruments to prepare Kacy to serve Christ. By the power of His Word, God molded a man He would use to reach broken and hurting people.

When we first met Kacy, he was the "funny guy" with a troubled past. If we had presented him with a list of things he needed to change about himself, Kacy may very well have complied—for a season. However, he would not have learned how to live independently from our close monitoring.

By contrast, waiting for the Lord to inwardly transform Kacy through the power of His Word prepared Kacy to think with the mind of Christ. The same holds true in parenting. Are you most concerned about getting your son to obey your list of rules? You may be able to coerce, manipulate, and threaten him to follow your standard, but if you have not taught your son from the Bible to think and live in obedience to God, he may one day flounder when he is out from under your watchful eye.

If your son is older and has not been grounded in the Bible, do not lose heart. Just as God changed Kacy, He is able to transform your son's thinking and mold him into a godly man. ...

The transformation in Kacy's life did not come because he "pulled himself up by his bootstraps" and willed himself to change. As his relationship with Christ matured, Kacy discovered how to respond when the Spirit convicted him of sinful thoughts and actions. Even today Kacy overcomes his troubled childhood memories by seeing himself through the gospel.

Kacy knows his heavenly Father's great mercy. God has caused Kacy to be born again to a living hope through the resurrection of Christ from the dead.

Kacy has been given a brand new life defined by what Christ has done. And with this promise, Kacy has inherited an imperishable inheritance reserved for him in heaven.

Teaching your son to apply God's Word to his life will provide him with a way to live victoriously—with a new identity in Christ:

Let the word of Christ dwell in you richly in all wisdom, teaching and admonishing one another in psalms and hymns and spiritual songs, singing with grace in your hearts to the Lord. (Colossians 3:16)

After I moved out of this young man's camper, he started leading worship more and more. He was succeeding in his calling and I was with the Stoppes. I lived on their couch now. They were counseling me, and helping make sense of the events I was going through. I was also trying to find work and, not long after, I did get a job and a car. I went from being homeless to being hired by Lake Travis High School to teach and coach basketball. Once again, I had a place of my own.

I honestly don't remember how long I lived with that young worship leader—probably only a few weeks. But after things got back on track for both of us, I learned that he had gotten a worship job in Seattle, Washington. His final night with us was at a Wednesday evening Bible study. He was leading worship with our teenagers; I was in the back listening, knowing it was his last night with us. After a couple of songs, he stopped and gave a short testimony. "About three or four months ago, I was going through the darkest time of my life," he said. "I was actually on the verge of suicide. And then, this guy moved in with me; he spent time with me and shared God's word with me; and I saw that God has a purpose and a plan for me. And now I know what that plan is."

I was standing in the back of the room, and I looked at Rhonda and asked, "WHO is he talking about?" And she literally slapped me on the arm, and snickered, "You! Stupid!" I was dumbfounded, "Oh! Talking about me? Oh, Shoot!" The whole time I was living at his house, God had been using ME to help him through this dark moment, and I had been lying on the couch whining, "God, why is this happening to me?" God was there during this whole process. He was pruning me. While he was using me to help this kid, he was also pruning me in preparation for the ministry he had planned for my life.

"I am the true vine, and my father is the gardener. He cuts off every branch in me that bears no fruit, while every branch that does bear fruit, he prunes, so that it will be even more fruitful. You are already clean because of the word I have spoken to you. Remain in me, as I also remain in you. No branch can bear fruit by itself; it must remain in the vine. Neither can you bear fruit unless you remain in me. I am the vine; you are the branches. If you remain in me and I in you, you will bear much fruit; apart from me you can do nothing. If you do not remain in me, you are like a branch that is thrown away and withers; such branches are picked up, thrown into the fire and burned. If you remain in me my words remain in you, ask whatever you wish, and it will be done for you."

~ John Chapter 15:1-7 (NIV)

God prunes us, and sometimes we don't even realize it. I'm not a gardener, I never was a gardener, I will never be a gardener, I know nothing about gardening - but I know about pruning. Pruning is this: It is trimming a tree, or shrub, or bush, by cutting away dead or overgrown branches or stems, especially to increase fruitfulness and growth. In order for plants to grow, they have to be cut. Like I said, I don't know anything about this stuff, other than that in my life, for sure, God had to cut away some things. Maybe it was pride or some other issue I was dealing with at that time, but he was cutting away. While I was lying on a couch in that travel trailer, He was pruning me.

Jesus says that God prunes the branches that BEAR fruit to allow the branches to bear MORE fruit. I love how the scripture reveals to us that God is pruning the branches that bear fruit. He already saw my potential. When I quit my job, I truly had done all that I was supposed to do; I was trying to live in God's will. I was just fine, and yet, He began to cut away to make me stronger and more useful in the work he had for me.

Vines left to themselves tend to sprawl in all directions and produce large canopies of leaves and branches. But they don't necessarily bear fruit. Pruning, therefore, is not a punishment. It is done so that the vine can be more productive—more fruitful. The thing is, when God prunes us (when He cuts on us), it's for our own good. Of course, it can hurt—just like the barbed wire fence that I had to get past to get into the pasture. It was a painful experience. But I knew I had to get through it.

I'd like to focus for a minute on that one verse in John

15: *"If you do not remain in Me you are like a branch that is thrown away and withers and is picked up and thrown into the fire…"*

I do think it is important to stop and consider what happens if you are NOT connected to the Vine. If you have a plane crash in life, and you are not connected to the vine, you're going to fall. You're going to hit the ground and you will be picked up and thrown into the fire. Basically, what this verse says is that if you're not connected to God, when the wind blows and things get rough, you won't be connected to anything and you will fall.

Here's a true-life story in which I saw this principle at work. My kids had been begging me to take them to a Christmas Tree Farm. I don't know if you've ever been to a Christmas tree farm, but at this point in my life, I didn't even know that there was such a thing as a Christmas tree farm. However, I agreed to go. We got there, a happy-go-lucky family on a big adventure to go cut down a tree for Christmas. I had never done this before in my life. But the kids were excited. There was a petting zoo and other fun stuff. And then, they handed me a saw, put us on a hayride, took us out to the woods, and said, "Find a tree. Cut it down. Drag it to the end of the road, and we'll pick you up."

I had never cut ANYTHING down with a saw. I had no idea what I was doing. Handing me a saw was a big mistake from the beginning. But, I went out there to do my fatherly Christmas duty.

The first tree the kids ran up to was this tiny little stick and they were squealing, "We want this one!" They had just watched the Charlie Brown Christmas Special about the little Charlie Brown tree. But I quickly put an end to that by stepping on the little tree. They were screaming, "NOOOOO!" But my wife saved the day by picking out a lovely tree that would fit just right in our living room. She announced, "This is what we want! Go, Daddy! Cut it down…" So, I dropped to my knees. I wanted to show my manliness. And I began to saw.

About 45 minutes later, I had gotten nowhere near conquering this tree. I could not get it cut down. I was struggling, the kids had lost interest (they were running around chasing each other), and my wife was standing by, just texting on her phone. I, on the other hand, was stuck underneath this tree. People were walking by singing Christmas carols, and I was yelling (at least, in my mind), "I hate Christmas!"

Finally, I was victorious. I cut this tree down, we

dragged it to the end of the road, we threw it on the truck, and we headed back up to the front to pay.

When we got there, some guy grabbed my tree and threw it on a machine which I had never seen before. He set the trunk firmly inside this box, and then stepped on a pedal and the entire tree just started shaking like crazy while the machine hummed along, "Brhhddddddudududududh." And I was about ready to go nuts myself. "Dude, what are you doing to my tree? It took me over an hour to cut that thing down!"

All of a sudden I was watching all of the pine needles that were not connected to "the vine"—not firmly attached to the branches—falling off and hitting the ground. Another guy, working with him, was raking up the pine needles, putting them in a wheelbarrow, rolling them down a hill and throwing them into a fire, and as I watched all this I was struck with the truth of the scripture, and I yelled, "John 15—that's John 15!!!" And the guy said, "No. My name's Michael." And I said, "Sorry," but I had to laugh as I watched.

I saw this take place and it was a huge illustration of John 15 to me. That tree was going through a storm. It was being violently shaken. Sometimes our lives get shaken up like that. Sometimes our lives get just spun out of control, and if we're not connected to that vine, we're going to fall, just like those pine needles. So it is important to remember what He says. "Remain in me and I'll remain in you." We've got to remain in Him. We never know what kind of storm we're going to face. We never know what kind of plane crash we're going to have to go through. We never know what obstacle we will have to get over. That's why it is so important to be connected to the Vine.

Maybe your pruning comes in the form of trying to kick a bad habit, or in sacrificing something, or dealing with a hidden sin. God only prunes stuff out of our lives that does not belong there. It's not going to be at all pretty (or fun), but here's what it is: productive. And, that's very good. Just as the tree that is pruned grows back even stronger than it was before, when God prunes us, we grow stronger spiritually. Don't miss the great big promise that's given in John 15:11: "These things I have spoken to you that My joy may be in you and that your joy may be made full (complete)." That is a huge promise! He wants us to have joy. He is not trying to hurt us or do anything bad to us; He's helping us grow stronger through whatever trial or obstacle it takes to prune us.

Romans 5:3-5 says: "More than that, we rejoice in our sufferings, knowing that suffering produces endurance, and endurance produces character, and character produces hope, and hope does not put us to shame, because God's love has been poured into our hearts through the Holy Spirit who has been given to us."

Be patient. Let Him work on you. From the time I accepted Christ as my Savior until the time I went through this monumental pruning process was around eight years. He knew the process I needed. He saw the "barbed wire fences" in my life that hindered me from reaching the goals and plans He had for me. And He was with me through the whole painful ordeal.

And so, if you are reading this, and you think that perhaps you are up against a barbed wire fence, getting slashed to pieces as you try to move forward—if there's some storm or crash that you are facing, please remember that God may be pruning you to bear more fruit in your life. It may hurt. It may sting. It may even leave scars. But you can push through if you put your trust in God. Don't give up hope. He is with you no matter what, and He will help you move through the painful experience to a better place.

My wife wrote the following poem that really spoke to me in my world. It is full of emotion and asks the questions that I had in my mind… but it helps us to realize that God is in control. He brings joy and peace.

He is Emmanuel - God with us.

Stolen

Stolen, robbed, abandoned,
Forgotten, ashamed, BITTER, ANGRY, empty

Empty like a …
Barren woman longing and hoping for the day she will amaze the doctors with news of conception.

Empty like ash on land… full of remains of a home that once had a firm foundation.
Ruined… by the flames of lust, addiction, greed, dead ends of a well run dry. I am thirsty.
I have tried everything this world has to offer, and still, I am empty, but why?? Why do I have a void that I cannot explain? Why is something still missing? Why am I left day in and day out…alone?

Night after night, my head hits the pillow like an ocean wave slamming into the jagged rock wall of a cliff. I toss and I turn unable to quench the overbearing thirst to numb my afflictions…

The thoughts in my head amplify...and drowned out
the peace I so long to feel that would allow me to sleep.
I cannot go on.

But there is a voice...
a voice calling my name with authority, a voice that
calms and brings peace...a voice that causes my heart to
beat out of my chest...a voice telling me I can go on.

I realize now that I need You. You are the Son of God...
You are my savior! I am a sheep, and You are my
Shepherd.... I am complete
and no one can take this away from me.

I am sorry...sorry I did not acknowledge You before.
It is You that has filled my emptiness. It is You that
makes all things new...new like a blank canvas ready to
become a masterpiece of the most skilled artist.

You have brought joy and peace to my world. You are
Emmanuel. God with me. You have stolen my heart.

Vickie Benson

CHAPTER 8

Rescued

*For the Lord says, "Because he loves me, I will rescue
him; I will make him great because he trusts my name.
When he calls on me, I will answer; I will be with him
in trouble and rescue him and honor him. I will satisfy
him with a long life and give him my salvation.
~ Psalm 91: 14-16 (TLB)*

I was losing hope. I was so far from home and apparently
from humanity. I was scared. I had felt every emotion
you could imagine at this point. And I felt like it was
starting to get dark. I kept hoping that somebody
would find us, but no one was in sight. The loneliness
that I had been feeling earlier just wrapped itself around
me as I realized it would soon be nighttime. There was
so much uncertainty. My grandpa was dead, and my

grandma was in and out. I wasn't even really sure she was still alive… and I knew I needed help. I needed help "BIG TIME!" How was anyone going to know where we were out in these woods? I felt so helpless and alone.

In desperation, I went out to the fence one last time in hopes of finding someone—anyone—who could help me. I had tried so many times. I had wandered for what seemed like hours. I was extremely thirsty, and the heat was unbearable. But this time, something was different.

I squeezed through the painful barbed wire fence once again. And as I stood there staring across the pasture, the thought overwhelmed me that I would not survive the night in these woods without help. And then something caught my eye. It was a light flickering through the trees. As I stared, I realized it wasn't one light—it was two. They were the headlights of a pickup truck.

"That's crazy," I thought. "I didn't even know there was a road down there." I thought I had scoured that entire pasture, but I had never noticed that road. But there it was, and at that moment the truck was slowly approaching the pasture. I'd been hoping to see something like this all day. Now was my chance—maybe my last hope. I couldn't let them pass me by!

I ran toward the truck. I remember the cows moving beside me. I guess they were thinking they were about to get fed. They ran with me, but I was not afraid like before. I ran right up to the front of the truck. I remember throwing my hands on the hood of the truck. I remember yelling "plane crash," pointing back toward the trees, and then I passed out! My desperate cry for help and to be rescued had been answered.

Fast-forward again to the scene of me going to move in with my dad. That was the beginning of another big crash. You cannot imagine how many times, as a speaker, I've met a teenager, who's just had a big blowout with their mom or dad and they say, "Oh yeah? Well, I'm just going to go live with Dad." (…or Mom, whichever is the other parent…) For some reason, we all have believed this will solve our problems. At least we will be getting out of an unhappy situation. Anytime I've ever shared my story about getting into a little argument with my mom, I've looked into the crowd and I see the many heads nodding in recognition. "M'hmm … Yep, I've been there!"

As I said earlier, when I left my mom to go live with my

dad, it went from one nightmare to another. He was drunk all the time, basically living in bars, and he didn't treat me any better than he treated himself.

On the first day of school, I learned pretty quickly that I was different from everybody else. I came from the city. After living in Galveston, Texas it was a culture shock to land in this "country town" of Benton, Louisiana where everyone spoke with funny accents. Up until then, I had never even heard of this place. Benton is a small town about 12 miles from Shreveport, with a population right around 2000.

When I first showed up at school, nobody really talked to me. I was very much alone; nobody wanted to have anything to do with me. People thought I was on drugs, because I was staying with my dad who had been smoking pot around me, and I would get high just from the contact. My clothes reeked of marijuana. I would get to school and face those hallways all by myself every day. The other kids would just look at me like I was an alien.

I WAS a little different. I was awkward and lanky. And my hair was way different than everybody else's. I had it cut in a Flock of Seagull's* mullet like you've never seen before. The front part was long and wavy with nicely cropped sides, and the back was even longer. It was pretty awesome, in my opinion, but not what was normal in the current setting.

(*Flock of Seagull's was a British Rock band popular in the 1980's. The mullet was a hairstyle, short on the sides and long in the back.)

That's what I came into. I walked into this school among strangers, and at home, I had this monster of an alcoholic father. I was alone, very scared, not knowing anybody. But then, one guy stepped out of his comfort zone.

He walked up to me as I was leaning against a wall, alone and friendless. No one in this place had ever yet tried to talk to me until this kid walked up. And the very first words out of his mouth were: "Hey are you a guy or a girl?" I was standing there with the coolest mullet you've ever seen, flicking my hair, and I just said, "Um... I'm a guy..." He quickly said to me, "Hey, I'm just kidding." I could have reacted badly to that, but honestly I was just happy somebody had said, "Hi." I could have punched the dude in the mouth, but I was at this place where I just needed somebody to reach out no matter what they said. His name was Brent and he was the son of a youth pastor. He just wanted to introduce himself and thought that would be a great way to do it. And I'm glad he stepped forward.

"I'd like you to come over and meet some of my friends," he said as he led me over and introduced me to what turned out to be the "church kids." I didn't know these people, and they didn't know me. They knew OF me; I'm sure they had seen me around. Almost right after he introduced me to his group, Brent invited me to church. And I said, "No. I don't do church."

There's a reason why I didn't want to go. A few years earlier, a "Christian" man in my life had abused the trust and responsibility that should be characteristic of the Christian name, and this left a bad taste or misunderstanding of what "church" was all about.

But rather than go into an explanation, I just said, "No" to Brent. I didn't want any part of church. I loved hanging out with him at school, though. I enjoyed his friendship. I enjoyed his liking me. He was just different—in a good way—and I noticed that right off the bat.

But he was persistent. He would ask over and over and over until at one point, I felt like saying, "Dude, quit asking!" I thought, "I'm going to have to fight guy if he keeps inviting me to church. I'm just going to punch him in the mouth." But eventually I did go.

Here's where he got me. He kept asking me to church… and kept asking me to church… and finally one day he told me they had free pizza. That got my attention. "What? Free pizza? Are you freaking kidding me? If you had told me that like a month ago, I probably would've showed up!!!"

One of the things I had been doing regularly was stealing crackers off the salad bar to take home with me. It was a kind of assurance to me that I'd have some kind of meal once I was at home. Sometimes my dad would get so drunk that he'd pass out for the evening. Or he'd leave and he wouldn't even be around at all. So, I didn't have food a lot of times, and that's why I would take those crackers home and stuff them in drawers, hiding them away for later. I was stocked up on crackers and I would eat them for dinner, for lunch, for breakfast, or whenever.

I used to make my own pizzas, just by putting a little ketchup on the cracker. So when this guy came up to me and said, "Hey, man, we've got free pizza," I was quick to respond. "All right. I'm down. Let's go…" This was kind of a big deal, so I went with him.

119

I didn't care about hearing anything about God or anything religious; I was going for the free pizza. Well, I got my pizza . . . and more. I started to make friends with these people, and that was a really cool feeling. So I kept going back. I didn't really listen much to the messages, although I'm sure they were good. I just enjoyed being there.

When I showed up for my free pizza, it was my first time to be in a church. I didn't get immediately "saved." I just listened and took it all in. Yet I saw something I'd never seen before. These people were different and I really enjoyed being around them. I already knew Brent was not like the kids I'd known. His father was the youth pastor, Wayne Craig. He and his wife Doreen were just incredible people. There was something about them that I'd never seen before. They later became like a family to me. When I first met them, I watched them closely. I saw how great they were with the students, and how nice they were to me. I thought they were all amazing, and there was always really cool stuff going on in that church. The best part about it was all the attention I was shown that I didn't ever get at home with my dad.

One day when I walked in, the kids were all excited because they were going somewhere. They had planned a field trip, and I had never been on a field trip. I didn't even know what a field trip was, but I was all in. They were eager to go, so they yelled to me to get in the van, and I said, "Are they gonna have pizza?" They laughed and said, "Yeah, we'll feed you. Let's go."

So I jumped in the van, and we all rode over to the mega church down the road called *First Baptist Church of Bossier City, Louisiana*. It was a huge church and apparently a big event. They had a special guest speaker, Jay Strack.

We were known to be the crazy youth group who always showed up late to everything, and we were always the loudest. True to form, we showed up at this church a little bit late, and we walked in the front entrance, causing a little distraction right there in front of everybody. People were shushing us, and I was being my natural loud self, calling out, "Hey we found it!" There was a guy up front praying, so I turned to my group to get their attention and let everyone know they needed to be quiet, "Oh no, they're praying! Everybody shut up!" We came in late, and so noisy, they sent us up to the very top of the balcony, in the very back of the building—so far back that my back was literally against the wall.

So, there I was. I didn't exactly care to hear anything that was happening. I was entertaining everybody— just being silly. I was kind of known for being the class clown. I guess I was trying to masquerade the pain I was going through by using humor. This was just a social event for me, nothing really spiritual. While they were playing the music, I was goofing off, and then suddenly Jay Strack took the stage.

As he began to talk, something about this man's manner... something about his voice... something about his demeanor... something about the words that were coming out of his mouth... something caught me off guard and blew me away. I had never heard anyone speak like that before, and it got my attention.

Then he started talking about how he grew up in a situation similar to mine, and his words grabbed ahold of me like nothing ever had. I really started to listen to this man. I listened to his whole story. I listened to what he said when he began to talk about Jesus.

I'd heard about Jesus, of course. I had heard Mr. Craig talk about this "Jesus" character many times, but never in my life had I put it together like this. It never had any impact on me before. But at the end of the night as this man brought out the message about salvation,

I began to see the light. I didn't know what salvation meant. I'd never even heard the word before.

And yet, when he started talking about having a relationship with Jesus, I began to have the strangest feeling, "I've got to get to know this Jesus; I need to know this Jesus." When I heard the man tell how Jesus can change a person's life, I felt it personally. "I need a changed life!" He said, "Listen. If you know someone who needs Jesus in their life, just stop and pray for them right now." And I remember looking over as every head in our youth group dropped in prayer and I wondered, "Who are they all praying for?"

Of course, they were all praying for me. Suddenly, the Holy Spirit hit me SO hard; I felt it in my chest. I needed this Jesus. The preacher said, "Listen, if you know that you need Jesus Christ in your life, I want you to come down here right now in front of me." I don't have a clue how I got down there. I don't remember what I did at that moment. I don't remember even getting up out of my seat, but moments later I was standing before this man who had been speaking all night, looking up at him with tears in my eyes, saying, "I NEED THIS LIFE CHANGE! I need to be rescued." It was like that moment after the plane crash when I knew I needed something. I knew I needed help—I needed to be rescued.

Just so, that night standing in front of the platform of that church in Bossier City, I had that understanding that I needed something. And as I looked up, the preacher said, "If you know you need Christ—you know you need Jesus in your life—I'm going to ask you to pray." He went through the gospel. He shared how God loves us so much, and I was in awe. I hadn't ever felt that kind of love. At home with my dad, I certainly didn't feel loved. But he told me, "God loves you so much he gave his life for you; God loves you so much he sent Jesus Christ to live on this earth to die for you." And that just absolutely blew me away. And I whispered, "I've just got to know this Jesus. I've got to have this."

I prayed that night. I fell on my knees for the first time to talk to God. I said, "Jesus, I don't know you, but I need you. I know that I need you and I can't live without you. I can't go through life without you. Come into my heart and rescue me from my sin and give me peace." I prayed that prayer and I was crying too. Tears were pouring out of my eyes. I was just bawling.

I had no idea why I was crying. I had no idea what was going on with me right then. I do know that every weight that I'd carried through my messed up life—from my failed relationship with my father, my arguments with my mother, even way back to the plane crash—everything you can imagine was weighing on top of me. But when I asked God to forgive me, to come into my life, to be my savior, and to rescue me, it all lifted. When I said "AMEN," I felt this incredible weight come off of me. I felt much lighter than I had ever felt before.

There were some beautiful stained glass windows in this church, and I remember looking up into this glass, my eyes watering from the tears, and it seemed as if the glass glimmered, as I felt every bit of my sin lift from me, and all the junk that had been weighing me down seemed to float through that glass. Jesus took it. He died for that, and He saved me. I knew that night I was finally rescued. It was the same feeling as I'd had when that truck pulled into that pasture long ago, and I knew I was saved and everything was going to be okay. That's what I felt in that moment on my knees when Jesus became real to me.

> "Therefore, if anyone is in Christ, the new creation has come: The old has gone, the new is here!
> ~ 2 Corinthians 5:17 (NIV)

The rest was a blur. They counseled with me. Then I met up with my youth group, they hugged me, they cheered me, and I still did not fully understand what was going on inside me, but I knew something good had happened. As I recall, I stayed the night with Brent and went to school the next day, as usual.

Afterwards, I went home and told my Dad about getting saved. Of course, he was drinking that night. And he became even more intoxicated as I tried to explain what had happened in my heart the night before. He got angry and a big fight followed. He hit me, he yelled at me, and he chased me into the woods, where I hid behind a tree—a familiar tree. I had hid behind that tree many times, but this time something different took place. This time I knew I wasn't alone. And I prayed for the second time in my life.

The previous night, I had prayed that God would come into my life and He became real to me. Now, I pleaded with my savior, "Jesus, I just met you, but I need help. I need help!" And for the first time in my life, I knew for sure that I was not alone. Even as I was hiding behind that tree with my out-of-control father stomping around nearby, I knew I was going to be okay.

I could hear my dad stumbling through the branches and yelling, until finally, he went inside and passed out. Soon, I also went inside and got in bed. When he woke up the next morning, he didn't remember any of it. That was the roughest part of these episodes. Typically, he'd get drunk and do wild and crazy things, but the next morning he would have no idea what had happened the night before. He didn't recall chasing me into the woods. He would not remember that he'd pulled a gun in my face. Or that he tried to hurt me. He had no idea. Every morning, I'd wake up remembering the terror, but he'd wake up seemingly unaware that anything had ever happened. He'd grab a beer, and the cycle would start all over again.

When I woke that morning, the cycle was broken for me; First, I had been rescued from my sin. And that night, I was rescued from my fear and loneliness the moment Jesus heard my pleas.

As I've mentioned, my dad would leave me at school a lot. I'd sit and wait and sometimes he'd pick me up real late, but sometimes not at all. And I would go sleep in the stairwell by the school, eat the crackers that I'd lifted from the salad bar, and get up in the morning and go to class.

Nobody even knew I'd been sleeping there. This was before they had cameras everywhere. And no one really checked on me at all. I'd be sitting in front of the school as the last person left, and they'd wave, "All right, see you later," while this kid remained out there in the schoolyard. That doesn't really happen much now.

On this occasion, it was nearly midnight and I'd been forgotten again. I was headed for my "bed" in the stairwell, when I looked up and saw something I had never noticed before. I had been stuck here many times, but on this night I spotted a light and it was over a phone booth.

I know that's not typical today, but back in the 80s there were phone booths in lots of places. Even schoolyards. As I saw the phone hanging there, I immediately thought about my grandmother. I knew that my grandmother loved me. I thought about how she had taken care of me so many times, and in that moment I decided to get up and use that phone to call grandma.

Hers is the one phone number that I can never forget in my whole entire life. Even today, I can remember her number, even though she doesn't use it anymore. I picked up the receiver and put it to my head. I knew her phone number by heart, but I didn't have any money. Fortunately, back then you could make "collect calls." I hit zero. A lady's voice came on the line. I said, "I've got to make a collect call to my grandmother. Here's the number…" When someone made a collect call, the operator would keep the caller on the line while they waited for the other person to answer, and then you could hear her ask the other party if they would accept (and pay for) the call.

It was midnight and I was trying to call my grandma. Would she answer the phone at this hour? And then I heard an old, but very dear voice on the other end of the line, croaking a sleepy "He-ellll-oh??" Then the operator (with as country a twang as you can imagine) said, "Ma-aam, I've got a collect call from your grandson, Kacy." I had told this woman I needed to call my grandma and apparently she could tell from my voice, the time of night, and my rapid explanation, that something serious was going on. So she patiently and urgently talked my grandmother awake.

Grandma couldn't hear me until we were connected, of course, but I could hear her, and I was yelling, "Grandma, grandma," but she didn't answer. Meanwhile, the operator was explaining, "Ma'am, there is a Kacy Benson on the other end of the line that needs you to accept a collect call." And I was begging, "Grandma, please accept this call." She finally got it and said, "Well of course!" And the lady said, "Well, here he is." (Obviously, she was aware that she was part of something critically important as she connected us. I could tell she was on my side.)

And then the voice at the other end of the line spoke to me. It was the incredible voice of my grandmother. And everything poured out. "Grandma. Dad left me at the school again. Can you come get me?"

I thought my grandma was incredibly old at the time. (Probably at least 40!) It was certainly not usual for her to be up travelling in the middle of the night. But, she didn't hesitate. "Of course." Where are you?" I was an hour away from her, if not more. But she said, "Sit tight. I'm coming to get you."

The hour dragged by. It was very quiet and nothing was going on out in the darkness. A little after 1 o 'clock a.m., I looked up to see lights coming down the road and I knew it must be grandma. She pulled up and I saw that my aunt (my dad's sister) was with her. Grandma grabbed my hand and said, "Get in the car." And I said, "Yes, ma'am." She said, "We're going to get your stuff; you're not staying there ANY more." And

I said, "Okay." Then I crumpled into the back seat of the car with relief.

We flew down the road and up to my dad's house and my grandma pulled up in the front yard; she did not bother to use the driveway—she literally pulled up onto the grass in front of the door. Then, she reached down and grabbed a pool stick. I don't know where she got it. I had not seen it before. But, this little woman grabbed that pool stick, turned to me, and said, "Let's go. We're getting your stuff." And I was thinking, "Oh. My. Gosh. This is happening."

She went up to the front door. She didn't knock; she didn't turn the knob. She literally kicked the door in. I stood on the porch, not wanting to move… I was frozen. She went inside and found my dad, laid up drunk in the bed with some woman. She kicked open the door to his room and started hitting him with the pool stick.

I could hear a great commotion. My grandma was swinging the pool stick around and shrieking, "You left my baby! You left my baby!" And he was yelling, "I don't know what you're talking about." And she kept whopping him with the pool stick. It was like a scene from "*Cops*." I had made my way into the room, when she turned around and pointed the pool stick at me, and said, "Get your stuff. We're getting out of here."

I grabbed what I could, threw it all into bags and ran toward the car. Meanwhile, grandma was backing people off with her stick. My dad was drunk and chasing us out. But my grandma kept letting him have it with the pool stick. All the while, she was running. I was running. My aunt was running. I dove into the back seat and shut the door. The others also jumped in, my grandma gunned it and we ended up doing donuts on the front lawn.

She ran over the yard gnome, the rosebushes, and anything else in her way. She didn't care. She took everything out. She spun around, hit the curb, hit the street, and went flying down the road. I looked at her expecting to see a maniac and it was just this little old lady looking up over the steering wheel.

I laid down in the back seat and I just started crying. It had been a very emotional time. Within a few days time I had just got saved spiritually, and I was still trying to figure all that out, when Grandma came to my rescue and stood up to my father in this crazy way. As I lay there weeping, she reached back. This was the same woman who was in the plane crash with me, the same woman who nearly died, the same woman who broke her back and was nearly cut in half by the seatbelt. She reached back and began to pat me on the back and as she patted my back, an incredible peace came over me. She said, "I've got you. I've got you and he's never going to hurt you again."

"But I trust in your unfailing love. I will rejoice because you have rescued me. I will sing to the LORD because he is good to me."
~ Psalm 13:5 (NLT)

I never went back to live with him. His life was up and down with drugs and alcohol until eventually his addictions killed him. But it was a critical point in my life when my grandma came to my rescue. I couldn't stay with her. I ended up going back to Galveston with my mom, and life did not magically get better. The struggles were real; there were problems that didn't just go away.

Just because we are rescued when we come to know Christ doesn't mean all our troubles disappear. But I learned, through all the stuff I went through, even after I'd gone home, that life IS a journey. Troubles and crashes in life are still going to happen. I know that I cannot make it without God's voice in my life.

Just as I had to be still in the woods and listen for my grandma so that I could figure out which way to go after the plane crash, I have to be still in life and listen for God. And He is always ready to give comfort and wisdom, no matter the circumstances.

The greatest moment of my life was not the day I was rescued from the plane crash. It was not the night I was rescued by my grandma. It was not being married, and it was not having kids. The greatest rescue story of my life was when Jesus became real to me. Choosing Him was the most important decision I've ever made. And that changed me forever.

Maybe you have been reading this book and you've had to face a crash in your own life. Or maybe Jesus has never been real to you. And maybe you have a feeling that you need help. If the cry of your heart is "I need to be rescued," then let me assure you that Jesus can rescue you. The Bible very clearly says that if you confess with your mouth, and believe in your heart that Jesus Christ is Lord, He will save you.

> *"If you openly declare that Jesus is Lord and believe in your heart that God raised him from the dead, you will be saved."* ~ *Romans 10:9 (NLT)*

You can even pray right now as you are reading this book. Simply call on him, "Jesus, I need you. I can't do this without you. I need you to rescue me. Forgive me of my sins. Come into my heart and be my savior." If you just prayed that prayer, and you meant it, your life is changed and you have been rescued. It doesn't mean that all of your problems will go away. If you know Jesus, then you can be assured that He will be with you through all of it. And from this day forward he will give you the strength, wisdom and courage to overcome your crash.

> *Is anyone crying for help? God is listening,*
> *ready to rescue you. If your heart is broken,*
> *you'll find god right there; if you're kicked*
> *in the gut, he'll help you catch your breath.*
> *~ Psalm 34:17-18 (MSG)*

Epilogue

Mac and Valerie Warren, along with their 7-year-old daughter Melissa, were relaxing outside on a hot Sunday afternoon. It was the 24th of July, 1977, and Summer was definitely at its peak. The Warrens joined several members of their extended family at the family's lake house on the western shores of Toledo Bend Reservoir in the Sabine National Forest. The nearest community was Huxley, Texas. Huxley is a quiet little place nestled deep in the piney woods of East Texas, where everyone knows everyone and close-knit families are common.

Church was over. Lunch was eaten. Everyone had gathered outside under a big shade tree beside the cabin to enjoy a peaceful afternoon overlooking the water. That's when they heard it. The lazy humming of a small plane overhead, fitting the mood of the day. Almost immediately, however, it became obvious that the little aircraft was in trouble. Mac looked up, searching the sky for the plane. He could see it was flying low, and could hear it making odd sputtering noises. And then it disappeared from view over a tree-line. The sound of the crash was loud, distinct and alarming. It was obviously a violent landing and whoever was in the small plane needed help immediately - if they were still alive.

The Huxley area was not highly populated so the Warrens feared they may have been the only ones who knew it had gone down, and could be the only ones who had any idea where it might be. As far as they could tell, the plane had crashed in a wooded area not far away. However, actually getting to the crash-site could be another matter entirely. They felt certain they could arrive before anyone else… assuming they could find it. Mac, Valerie, her father Billie Joe O'Rear, her brother Sammy O'Rear, and a few other family members would be the first responders.

Mac worked for the Deep East Texas Electric Cooperative, and he had his work truck with him at the cabin that weekend. Valerie grabbed 7-year old Melissa, and they all jumped in the truck. They sped out onto the highway, and turned onto a forest service road, rushing in the direction of the crash.

Being in a national forest, there were trees everywhere. As the Warrens began their search, they scanned the sky for signs of smoke from a possible fire - but didn't find any. Next, they checked a few properties on the main road but still didn't find anything. After some more searching, they made their way onto a large parcel of property owned by a local family (that family still owns, farms, and lives on the property to this day). They had lots of timber but also had some pasture... where they raised cattle.

As they drove through the farm and went through one cattle gate after another, they kept their eyes open, searching for signs of the crash. They made their way past a tall stand of timber on their right and turned through another gate into a pasture. As soon as they reached the clearing, they saw something very out of place - a little boy, all alone in the pasture - and he was running as fast as he possibly could, straight toward their truck.

The little boy, of course, was Kacy. When he reached the truck he slammed his hands on the side of it, yelled "plane crash" while pointing toward the trees, and crumpled to the ground in obvious exhaustion.
Mac jumped out of the truck, grabbed him and pulled him up into the cab with them. Kacy was scratched

up, forlorn, and seemed terrified. They weren't sure if he was okay at all. But he began asking questions. He wanted to know if the cows were going to hurt him. Mac assured him that they would not. He let them know that he was from Galveston and had never seen cows before. It seemed that he was more scared of the cows than he was that the plane had crashed. Mac and Valerie were heartbroken that this precious child had endured such an awful experience.

They all looked in the direction he had pointed toward the crash, but all they saw was a dense tree-line at the edge of the pasture. Sammy O'Rear, and his father Billie Joe, began making their way through the woods toward the site of the crash, in hopes of finding more survivors. Mac and Valerie, along with little Melissa, focused their attention on taking care of the little boy.

Kacy was hungry and thirsty. On the back of his work truck, Mac carried a water cooler with the little paper cups attached. So there was always drinking water available. A child herself, Melissa sensed the shock of the moment and hurried to get Kacy a cup of water. Having her there seemed to put him more at ease. Somehow having a younger person, someone close to his age, was comforting.

The boy kept asking about his grandparents. He was very concerned about them. By this time, Billie Joe & Sammy had reached the wreckage. From what they saw, they believed both grandparents were certainly deceased. Although they never went into the woods to see the remnants of the plane, Mac and Valerie assumed the same thing.

So the Warrens focused on sheltering Kacy from seeing or overhearing any bad news, such as the deaths of both his grandparents. Billie Joe had come back out of the woods and delivered the bad news – believing both grandparents were deceased.

Because his truck was equipped with a two-way radio, Mac was able to call for help and the authorities were soon on their way. The Sheriff had already contacted the FAA. The nearest airport in Center, Texas, is very small, but they had contacted some pilots in the community who could possibly get in their planes and hit the air to try to locate the crash. In the end, that was unnecessary.

Such news gets around fast in a small town. Apparently, there were a number of people who heard the plane in distress. The word was getting around among the locals that something had happened and many others began showing up at the site. Eventually, the owners of the land had to stop people from entering their property because there were so many.

It didn't take much longer for the sheriff to arrive. Mac and Valerie didn't take in all the details about the rescuers because they were so focused on taking care of Kacy, holding him close. Once they made that radio call and knew help was on the way, they knew there wasn't much more they could do; but they felt compelled to "be there" for this poor little boy. Eventually, they released him into the hands of officials, so he could accompany his grandmother on an ambulance to Shreveport.

The lights of the emergency vehicles disappeared down the road that evening, and that seemed to be the end of the story for the Warrens & O'Rears. A local man and his wife were hired by the FAA to guard the plane overnight, until they could arrive and continue the investigation the next day. But aside from a short article in the local newspaper, there was no further information for the couple to follow. They didn't learn that the grandmother had survived. They didn't know how to get in touch with the injured family to follow up. And, if Kacy had told them his name, they didn't remember it. They referred to him in the retelling of the story simply as "the little boy from the plane crash." Occasionally throughout the years, the story would come up in conversation… but there was never a way to follow up or see what had become of him—and no contact.

Fast forward 4 decades. Mac and Valerie had raised their family, were retired and still living in the area. Melissa was grown, had a family of her own, and had given Mac and Valerie some beautiful grandchildren. the crash was a distant memory. But then one day, Valerie received a phone call. It was October of 2015—just over 38 years since that hot summer day. She learned that someone was looking for the people who had rescued that little boy so long ago. And an exciting reunion would soon follow!

In Valerie's words, "It's been such a blessing for us to meet Kacy again… it was quite a surprise when we got the phone call from Mac's brother, Larry Warren, letting us know that David King had contacted him!" David, who manages Kacy's ministry, contacted Larry in an effort to track down Kacy's rescuers. Several months later, following an earlier reunion, Kacy and David made their way to East Texas for a visit. While there, the Warrens took them to the farm to visit the actual scene of the crash.

It was an exciting and surreal experience for Kacy to return to that field on the edge of the woods after so many years. Some things looked the same but lots of things had also changed. He spent long minutes attempting to reconnect old memories to a place that looked similar but also very different. Since the crash, Kacy had found Christ, grown up, gotten married, and now had children of his own. His youngest, Tyton, was with him that day.

Following that visit, Mac commented, "He (Kacy) always thought that we rescued him, but we didn't feel like we were doing anything; we just showed up. It could have been anybody, you know. We just happened to be the first ones there and took care of him." After all those years, it also came as a surprise to Mac and Valerie that Kacy's grandmother was still alive and well, at the age of 89.

Shortly after David King had initially located The Warrens by phone, Valerie called her daughter Melissa to share the news. Melissa was very excited! "Mom called me and said you won't believe this! When she told me about the phone call and that his name was Kacy Benson, I went to see if I could find him on Facebook. I was very excited and wanted to know more, so I found his profile and sent a friend request. Then I saw that he had recently spoken at a church near my home. I also saw on Facebook that a friend of mine, who attends that same church, was a mutual friend with Kacy! So I asked if she knew of Kacy Benson. She replied that she had heard him speak and loved hearing him! And…when he spoke that night at her church, he had actually told the story of the crash! I said, 'You will not believe this! I was there that day.' And then I told her the whole story."

Not long after reconnecting with Kacy by Facebook, Melissa learned that he was coming back to speak at that same church near her home. The whole family agreed they just had to go and meet him again. So, Mac, Valerie, Melissa & Sammy (Billie Joe had since passed away) all made the drive to Longview, Texas, for the long-awaited reunion. And, they all got to hear him deliver a message about our Savior. Being Believers themselves, it was an amazing evening.

The family had wondered for all those years what had happened to the little boy they met that day running scared from a plane crash. During the course of the evening, a lot of those questions were answered. Kacy gave his testimony. He told of the things that he had been through, both in the crash and other aspects of his life, such as his experiences on the streets and with his Dad, as you have read about in this book. That night a group of students gave their lives to Christ.

The family was amazed. God definitely had a purpose for preserving that little boy, and had an amazing plan for his life. As Mac said, "We don't always understand why things work out like they do, but often there are reasons that we cannot see."

Shaking hands with Kacy, at the end of the evening, Sammy O'Rear summed it up nicely. "Now I know why we found you!"

Finding the Rescuers

My name is David King. Kacy Benson and I have been friends (more like brothers) since 1992. We met one night when I was a police officer in Houston, Texas. He was a wayward young man who had previously given his heart to Christ, but he wasn't exactly living for Him at the time. About midnight, as I was driving my patrol car through a nightclub parking lot, I first spotted Kacy and a friend...juggling. They were doing their best to attract attention and impress the girls. I don't recall whether they were having any success with the girls, but they were definitely making a spectacle. I was amused and stopped to say "hello." We've been friends ever since.

Some time later, as he grew closer to the Lord, Kacy and I spent more than a decade traveling the country together producing summer church camps. It was an incredible experience. During those years we saw thousands of students come to know Christ. As of this writing in April of 2016, I manage Kacy's speaking ministry. And, as his manager, it was my job to help him turn a long-ago experience into this book. That's how I came to be involved in this story.

In October of 2015, Kacy began to share his vision for the book with me, and told me the story of The Crash in detail. Although we had been friends for years, I knew very little about all that had happened that day. He spoke about fuzzy memories of the nameless strangers who had found him, a tiny little boy, sitting all alone in that field on the edge of the woods. He remembered a family that drove up in their truck. When he saw them, he ran toward the truck out of sheer desperation. And then, just as his hands touched the hood of their vehicle, he fainted. He remembered being in the truck later with the little girl giving him water as rescue workers tended to his grandmother. The last thing he said was how much he would love to find those people and express his sincere thanks for all they had done.

As I listened to Kacy tell the story, I realized the final chapter of this book was missing. We needed to find those people. After that day, Kacy had never again seen or spoken to them and, naturally, had no idea who they were. But, I felt compelled to find them and bring the story full-circle….and, hopefully, have some kind of reunion. But we had no idea who they were, if any of them were still in the area, or if they would even be willing to talk if we could find them. For all we knew, after almost 40 years, they could have been scattered to the wind. I only knew I had to try.

For 38 years, Kacy had tried to locate news or information on The Crash. There were no known photos, no articles, no documents, and no witness accounts—nothing. Since it happened when he was so young, and due to the trauma, his memories of that day were hazy. My goal was to find a photo of the crashed plane, maybe a copy of the Federal Aviation Administration (FAA) investigation, or perhaps an old newspaper article to include in this book. Of course, locating and reconnecting Kacy with his rescuers was the ultimate goal. However, starting with so little information, and after 4 decades had passed, I was less than optimistic.

I began my research with the only sliver of a clue Kacy's family had. It was a copy of an old letter from a law firm in Dallas. It referenced a payment to a company for some photographs they had taken of the crash scene.

The letter was addressed to a company in New Jersey, which had apparently taken the photos on behalf of the FAA. I really hoped to get a copy of those photos!

First I contacted the law firm. But they no longer had any records, files or pictures from so long ago. Next I tried to locate the company in New Jersey that took the photos. But as far as I could tell, it no longer exists. So, the FAA was my last hope from this lead. I found The Crash listed in their online database so there was some hope. I emailed their offices in Washington, D.C., inquiring about any photos or records they might have of the crash which occurred in 1977. Surprisingly, it only took them a week or so to respond. Incredibly, their reply said that all of their crash records prior to 1978 had been destroyed. 1978. Seriously? We missed the cutoff by a single year?!? I couldn't believe it. The letter was a complete dead end. On to the next idea.

Coincidentally, some of my own ancestors who had come to Texas in the early 1800's, had settled in Shelby County—the same county where The Crash had occurred. In fact, some members of my extended family still live there today. Because of that, I was aware that Shelby County had a Historical Society located in the town of Center, which is not far from the crash site. So, I sent an email asking if they might have any information on the crash. For several days, I heard nothing back. No response at all. But about 10 days later, I got some news.

A dear, sweet lady named Reecie Stanley (known locally as Ms. Reecie) from the Shelby County Historical Society emailed back. In short, she had taken a personal interest in helping us. Ms. Reecie had already spoken with the Shelby County Sheriff's office—but they had no records of the crash. Fortunately, she was not ready to quit.

'The Light and Champion' is a local paper that covers all of the major events in Shelby County. Their slogan is "Covering Shelby County like the Pine Straw Covers the Ground." Back in 1977, it was simply called "The East Texas Light." Although the small paper doesn't usually reply to research requests for old editions, Ms. Reecie somehow got her hands on the archives. She searched for any records of The Crash. And there it was.

In here email reply, Ms. Reecie said that she had located the newspaper headline telling the story of the crash. It included a grainy photo of the mangled plane, and the names of the people who found Kacy that day. The article listed his name as K.C. She said she was mailing a copy of it, but it would take a day or two for me to receive it. Of course, being so excited, I was not willing to wait and called her immediately.

When she and I connected by phone, she said the man that found Kacy was named Larry Warren...a man she knew personally! I was shocked to finally have a name. She went on to say that Larry worked at the local electrical co-op and I could simply call him there. She even had the phone number! Again, I was elated! I felt certain I was almost there. But, when I called the co-op, they said Larry had retired. When I asked if they knew any way that I might locate him, they freely gave me his home telephone number. I guess the paranoia regarding 'privacy of personal information' hadn't yet reached all the way into East Texas. But, I wasn't complaining!

Next, I called Mr. Warren's home, and got his voicemail. Still unsure if I was even contacting the right person (and a bit skeptical), I left a detailed message about why I was calling. But, due to my big-city cynicism, I doubted I would ever hear anything back. A voicemail from a stranger, about an accident that happened 40 years prior, seemed like a great reason for Mr. Warren to hit the delete button and forget I had ever called. Fortunately, he didn't share my cynicism about telephone calls from strangers.

About an hour later, my iPhone lit up with a call. Again, I was elated; but, it was short-lived. Mr. Warren was very nice and more than willing to talk with me. However, he had no recollection at all of the crash and absolutely no idea who Kacy was or what I was talking about. He spoke with his wife, who also had no memory of a plane crash. After seemingly coming so close, I had hit another dead end. Completely deflated, I thanked him for his time and for returning the call of a stranger. Apparently, that trail had also ended, but at least we had the article Ms. Reecie was sending. Oh, well.

I had to accept the fact that I might never find the people involved. There was work to be done that day and I had to stop thinking about my search and get busy on other things. Another hour or so went by and my mind had completely moved on to other things. Then my iPhone lit up again. When I glanced over and saw that it was Larry, my heart literally jumped. I thought maybe he had bumped his head or had some epiphany that had jogged his memory. Either way, I was eager to hear from him again.

When I answered, Larry blurted out the news like we

were old friends. "David! I figured it out! It was my brother, Mac Warren, that found the crashed plane. I just spoke with him and he said he's always wondered what happened to that little boy from the plane crash. He can't wait to talk to Kacy!" After all the emotional ups and downs in my searching, I was stunned! I couldn't believe what I was hearing. I had found them.

I asked Larry if I could put him on hold for a moment. I quickly dialed Kacy who was in the shower when he answered. Who answers a cell phone in the shower!?. But, I was undeterred. I told him to grab a towel because I had a conference call he HAD to take immediately. He tried to persuade me to call back after his shower, but I refused to wait. I hit the button to merge the two calls. Of course, I let Larry deliver the news to Kacy that we had found the people who rescued him and his grandmother four decades earlier. The search was over.

In the Fall of 2015, the Warren family and Kacy met at one of his speaking engagements. It was the first time any of them had seen Kacy since 1977. Following his message that evening, several students gave their lives to the Lord. The Warren's were elated. Not only were they Kacy's rescuers…they were also followers of Christ, and were excited to see God using his life in such an amazing way.

About 6 months later in April of 2016, Kacy and I visited the Warren's in Shelby County. They drove us out to the farm and we spent some time visiting where it had all happened. The previous year, I had told Ms. Reecie that we would be coming to town for a reunion with the Warrens. She was excited at the prospect and requested that Kacy and I come to visit her when we came to town. Sadly, when I asked where we might find her, we learned that she had since passed away. And to this day, no one at the newspaper or the historical society can say exactly where or how she found that newspaper article.

Thank you, Ms. Reecie. We are forever grateful.

That was my small contribution to completing this story that spanned four decades, two families, and an incredible tragedy involving a little boy.

I met that little boy 15 years after The Crash, juggling in a parking lot. Who knew?

East Texas Light

*"Covering Shelby County
Like The Pine Straw Covers The Ground"*

Wednesday, July 27, 1977 Edition

A plane crash near Huxley Sunday claimed the life of a 47-year-old Springhill, Louisiana man, James W. Benson. Mrs. Benson was seriously injured in the crash and was transferred to Confederate Memorial Hospital in Shreveport with back injuries. The couple's six-year-old grandson, K.C. Benson was also a passenger in the plane, but the boy escaped with only minor injuries. James was pronounced dead at Memorial Hospital in Center by Dr. Joe Hooker.

The crash was reported to the sheriff's office about 3:30 Sunday afternoon by Huxley residents who heard the plane's engine quit, then heard the sound of the crash.

Game Warden Mike Warren and State Trooper James Moore went to the area to begin a search for the plane, while Sheriff Ben Samford recruited local pilots J.M. Ward, Ray Sancton and Byron McDaniel to search firm the air.

Mac Warren, a service man for the Deep East Texas Electric Coop, joined the ground search and was the first to find the plane after talking with a fisherman about the direction the plane was flying. The ground search party met with the little boy, K.C. Benson, who had left the plane to go find help.

The plane, a single engine Mooney, crashed in a wooded area near an open field where the pilot may have been attempting to land after the engine quit.

An inspection team from the Federal Aviation Authority conducted an investigation at the scene Monday. The

158

FAA Inspector engaged James Owens of Huxley to guard the crashed plane until the inspection team arrived. FAA Chief George Seaberg in Shreveport said Tuesday an inspection team has not been able to definitely pin-point the cause of the plane crash, but determined that the pilot and owner of the plane, James Benson, was attempting to make a forced landing in a pasture, but overshot the pasture and crashed into the trees instead. The reason for the forced landing has not been determined, but inspectors suspect engine trouble.

The Federal Aviation Official said Benson was apparently a well-qualified pilot, and the plane met federal licensing requirements. He said the "E-L-T" Unit, or emergency location transmitter, which is required, was installed and functioning properly. The E-L-T transmits an emergency radio beacon signal in case a plane crashes in a remote area, and sends this signal on an emergency frequency of 121.5 Megahertz which can be traced with directional receivers. The device is activated by the impact of the crash, and Seabert said it was operating after the crash at Huxley.

But Seaberg said it was not necessary to use the directional receivers to locate Benson's aircraft since the location was fairly well pinpointed by residents who heard the crash, and said local officers and ambulances reached the scene as quickly as could be expected under any circumstances.

CPSIA information can be obtained
at www.ICGtesting.com
Printed in the USA
LVOW04s1016060816
499243LV00010B/22/P